Praise fo

MW00581036

The most important word in all of fundraising has just four letters: CARE. Not give, not help, not work. CARE is the emotional, rational superglue that attracts donors and keeps them close. John Haydon's legacy with this book is telling nonprofits that they must care about the donors they have and have had in the past. He explains how to care for donors with simplicity as well as urgency. Anyone who likes your organization enough to give to it, to help, to work for you—they care most about your cause. Care back or you will lose them.

—Jim Greenfield, ACFRE, AFP Distinguished Fellow,
co-author of *Major Donors: Finding Big Gifts
in Your Database and Online* and a dozen other titles

You've found it! A powerful roadmap for nonprofit fundraising success. John Haydon has always had important things to teach our sector. But this book is overflowing with actionable tactics and a whole lot of common sense. When you implement John's candid and very personal advice—be prepared for unimaginable growth!

—Lori L. Jacobwith, founder, Ignited Fundraising,
fundraising culture change expert and master storyteller

This book is a gift to you. And one you should gift to every fundraiser you know. It will transform the way we do fundraising. And in the process, this will mean billions more in donations to improve our world.

—Harvey McKinnon, co-author of *The Power of Giving*

Put to immediate use—with joy and action—John's final gift for the nonprofit sector he loves. What you'll find on these pages is proven, practical advice on what it truly takes to keep your donors happy. It's a towering legacy containing John's lifetime of precious knowledge for every fundraiser who wants their cause to prosper and grow.

—Lisa Sargent, international fundraising copywriter and donor retention communications expert

If your work is in any way funded by donors, get this book. And buy a copy for each of your board members and staff. They all need to understand the donor concepts here. John's wisdom will have you raising all the money your nonprofit deserves!

—Marc A. Pitman, CFCC, Concord Leadership Group LLC and author of *Ask Without Fear!*

Donor retention is where it's at and this book will help nonprofits look at retention in a different (and better!) way. What a wonderful gift, what a tremendous legacy to leave us to work with for many years to come.

—Erica Waasdorp, president, A Direct Solution, and author of *Monthly Giving: The Sleeping Giant*

Donors are the gorgeous people whose love and passion, generosity and faith, make charity possible. John built this entire book around these lovely strangers. It's an easy read, portraying some complex principles in an accessible way. This well-researched, fact-based book is essential for any new fundraiser and their bosses if they really want to understand why they need to keep donors and how to do just that.

—Sean Triner, co-founder, Moceanic (global) and Pareto Fundraising (Australia)

John Haydon's book is a must-have for every fundraiser! His Donor CARE framework demonstrates how fundraisers can and must create deeper donor relationships, leading to greater engagement, retention, and giving. Full of data, real-world examples, stories, and his own inspiration, every fundraiser can use the strategies that John freely shares no matter where she is in her career. John's insights deliver the expertise and authentic connection donors everywhere need and require.

—Beth Ann Locke, Chief Spark, The Fundraiser Coach

Benjamin Franklin once said, "If you would not be forgotten . . . either write things worth reading or do things worth writing." John Haydon has done both! There is no way to put a price tag on the value of the information I've gained as a result of John's work.

—Michelle Sanders Brinson, Communications and PR Manager, Nashville Rescue Mission

The cure for the misplaced obsession over donor acquisition lies in building donor loyalty after the first gift. The true path to success is to keep donors coming back. John Haydon has devoted his career to advising on practical ways to increase donor loyalty and commitment. I marvel at his generosity. He then spent the final months of his life getting his decades of great advice down on paper. Donor CARE *is John's everlasting gift to us all.*

—Roger Craver, editor-in-chief, The Agitator and author of *Retention Fundraising: The New Art and Science of Keeping Your Donors for Life*

Publisher's Note

When we learned John's cancer was terminal, we discussed donating book proceeds beyond his author royalties to John's son, Guthrie. With John's blessing, Bold & Bright Media is sharing 50 percent of the book proceeds with Guthrie's trust. Under the light of a full moon, John passed away quietly and peacefully on February 8, 2020.

Antionette Kerr and Kivi Leroux Miller
March 2020

DONOR

CARE

How to Keep Donors Coming

Back after the First Gift

DONOR CARE

How to Keep Donors Coming

Back after the First Gift

JOHN HAYDON

BOLD & BRIGHT
M E D I A

Copyright © 2020 John Haydon

Published by Bold & Bright Media, LLC.
319 Becks Church Road
Lexington, North Carolina 27292
Boldandbrightmedia.com

No portions of this publication may be reproduced, distributed, transmitted, stored, performed, displayed, adapted or used in any form or manner without prior written permission, except for certain limited non-commercial uses permitted by the United States Copyright Act, such as brief quotations embodied in critical reviews.

ISBN-13: 978-0-578-64182-9

Library of Congress Control Number: 2020933877

Bold & Bright Media is a multimedia publishing company committed to bold hearts, bright minds, and storytellers whose experiences will inspire and compel others to grow in their own greatness. For more information visit BoldandBrightMedia.com.

Contents

Part Two: CONNECT

Part Three: APPRECIATE

Part Five: ENCOURAGE

Part Six: SURROUNDING YOURSELF WITH CARE

Foreword

Dear reader, please know:

You are John Haydon's legacy.

John wrote this "everything I know" book while undergoing chemo and radiation and suffering and anxiety and Buddhist-inspired realization.

For over two years, John Haydon fought metastatic cancer. He fought it for his cherished (compassionate and much taller) teenage son, Guthrie. John fought it for his long-time love, Kate. He fought it for his half-wild dog companion, Otis.

And John fought it for you . . . he really did. "I love nonprofits," as you will read.

On December 12, 2017, when first diagnosed, John started a Facebook group called "Watch John Beat Cancer." He expected to triumph.

Instead, you have this book.

In this book, you'll learn about John Haydon's revolutionary CARE framework for donor communications.

John wanted his CARE framework to be his special legacy to the nonprofit world he loved . . . but, in fact, *that's up to you.*

If you improve your donor retention because you adopted the CARE framework, then John will have his legacy.

If you improve your donor's average gift size because you adopted his CARE framework, then he will have his legacy.

If you improve your donor's lifetime value because you adopted John's CARE framework, then he will have his legacy.

If your donors, thanks to John's CARE framework, learn to like and enjoy and fully trust and even identify with your charity as a member of a family . . . then John will have his legacy.

If you knew John as a consultant, you probably knew him mostly for his work in the digital realm. But the CARE framework applies to ALL donor communications: digital, print, in person; *whenever* you speak with your donors.

CARE stands for something profound: their **Connection** with a good purpose—the mission and vision of your nonprofit—matters; your **Appreciation** of donors matters; your reporting about impact while encouraging donors to **Reply**—to speak with you—matters; and your **Encouragement** of the donors' growing commitment matters.

Love matters most. Your love for your supporters.

The revolution is in your hands now.

With sorrow (for John), with thanks (for all his new book taught me), and with hope (for his legacy, through you; and for the improved sustainability of the nonprofit sector, needed more every minute by our suffering world) . . .

Tom Ahern

PREFACE

Cancer Wrote This Book

I never thought it would happen to me.

I ate well, worked out three times a week, and aced my physicals. My stellar health (and babyface) belied my age, which often surprised people who asked. So you can imagine how terrified I was when one Saturday in December 2017, I discovered a small lump just above my left collarbone.

When a Roll of Cookie Dough Isn't a Good Thing

An MRI revealed a surprisingly large tumor in my chest, the size of a roll of cookie dough. Seven oncologists from the top cancer hospitals in Boston entered the examination room (never a good sign). Their expressions revealed more curiosity than concern about how it was possible for someone with such a large tumor to be walking and talking with absolutely no symptoms. I literally had no idea that I had cancer, much less a massive tumor sandwiched between my heart and lungs.

I thought about the many dog friends I hold near and dear who have lumps and bumps—tumors on butts, shoulders, necks, all over—and they seem as happy as ever. Why would I feel any differently if there's no pain?

My attitude was determined, almost joyful, to win no matter what. Like, "Watch me, cancer! I'm going to win." I felt that my will to live had to be bigger than cancer's will to kill me. So I bolstered my will to live.

I decided I had to write my cancer story; otherwise, the cancer would write it. I had to write it, direct it, and even take the leading role as me—the hero who beat cancer by not giving up no matter how bleak things looked.

I also needed my friends more than ever, so I started a Facebook Group in December of 2017 called "Watch John Beat Cancer." This was a way for me to put a specific and wildly positive intention out into the universe ("Watch me!") with the love and support of my friends. I knew I could beat cancer if I had friends cheering me on, sharing their cancer stories, or sharing a GIF just when I needed it most. But the best part is seeing people make new friends through this group.

At the same time, I was also terrified that I would die. Scared that my teenage son would have to grow up without a father. Terrified that I would never see him graduate high school. Terrified that I would have lived a life of "quiet desperation," leaving nothing behind except for a fading mention in the Boston Globe obituaries.

I thought about the things that mattered, that really mattered. Of course, friends and family came first to my mind. My son; my girlfriend, Kate; my two brothers, Jim and Bill; my nephews; and other extended family and friends (see the Acknowledgments for the big list).

But there was also my professional legacy. What would I leave behind as a lasting monument that would represent my work, my experience, and my expertise? After all, while doing this work for over 12 years, I've received countless emails from people thanking me for changing the way they approached marketing and fundraising.

When I shared my cancer story on Facebook, colleagues also validated my contribution. I heard comments like, "You're a name brand in this space. Orgs need you, and our field has benefited so much from all you've given it." Comments like these made me realize that I had to do something to repay my debt of gratitude to so many nonprofit marketers and fundraisers. Without them, I couldn't have contributed in such a substantive way.

So I started seriously thinking about this question day and night. How could I leave behind a record of the experiences I've had for the past 12 years? I pondered. I prayed.

During long days of chemo, as I wracked my brain for a way to distill all the remarkable experiences into a single record, I also thought to myself: What is the number problem one I'd love to solve?

One particularly vexing problem I've encountered over and over again is the unintentional lack of donor care, reflected in poor retention rates and lowered expectations of donors in the sector. And since building positive relationships with donors is one of the best ways to ensure sustainability for your nonprofit, I've sought to tackle this problem in this book.

So here you have it. If this is the last book I ever write, let it be known that Donor CARE contains the essence of what I've learned and taught about keeping donors happy during my brief but wonderful experience working with people who are making the world a better place.

John Haydon
January 2020

Acknowledgments

People I Owe, Big Time

You wrote this book.

I love nonprofits. I can say without hesitation that you have devoted your time, talent, and energy to something that matters. You are committed to important work—work that is bigger than yourself. A life without this kind of purpose is not a life well-lived.

You create beauty, gain, and good.

The impact that you make every day creates a beautiful world. You enhance the beauty and inherent dignity in people's lives. With your compassion, you turn suffering into healing, hopelessness into opportunity, loss into success. Without a doubt, you improve the quality of life in your community. All these things create a beautiful world.

Through your fundraising efforts, you create a sustainable organization. Revenue fuels your programs and projects. And, in turn, you should gain a fair and commensurate income. You should be able to pay your bills, save for your future, and live a comfortable life. Just because you help people doesn't mean you should sacrifice your own well-being. It's the opposite, in fact: you give so much of yourself that you should make a good living.

You create good. Your hard work makes people's lives better. You fight for equality, combat injustice, provide food and other essentials, and give reassurance during a crisis. That's you, unleashing goodness into the world. Thank you for making the world less scary, less lonely, and more hopeful for so many people.

The Small Village That Barn-Raised This Book

Specifically, I must thank the following people for making this book a reality. They often had more hope than me in getting this sandwich out the door. (*Sandwich* is what I call books that offer nutrition we all need: hope, healing, connectedness, gratitude, and courage.)

Kate Rubin—My Toad, my lover, my friend. Your care is woven here, as it's been woven in me.

Guthrie Haydon—My son, who many years ago implored me with his innocence to do meaningful work. He was only a four-year-old at the time, so his spirit, not his words, conveyed what I needed to hear.

Joe Waters—My brother from another mother whose enduring friendship carried me through writing this book and eventually the most difficult task we all have to face at some point in our lives.

Tom Ahern—Whose mentorship and love gave life to the vision for this book and an understanding that fundraising is much more about love than raising.

Julie Cooper—Whose steadfast hand and steady support renewed my belief in this book when I often lost faith.

Kivi Leroux Miller—My humble mentor who provided much needed humor in the most difficult times.

The Crowd That Shouted from the Rooftops

Here they are in no particular order, and certainly not in order of importance:

Tony Arnold	Adrian Sargeant	Amy Eisenstein
Ian Adair	Shana Masterson	Jerold Panas
Leah Eustace	Meico Whitlock	Penelope Burk
Josh Hirsch	Chris Strub	Andrea Kihlstedt
Robin Carton	Bill Sayre	Michael Rosen
Kirsten Bullock	T. Clay Buck	Kris Putnam-Walkerly
Erica Waasdorp	Debbie Merriam	Pamela Grow
Simone Joyaux	James Haydon	Miriam Brosseau
Jeff Brooks	Laura Haydon	Jean Wilcox
Mark Phillips	George Weiner	Rob Cottingham
Lisa Sargent	Harvey McKinnon	Gail Perry
Simon Scriver	Christine Egger	Julie Edwards
Chris Baylis	Lynne Wester	Steven Shattuck
Scott Ayers	Beth Kanter	Chris Brogan
Daisaku Ikeda	Roger Craver	Dennis Fischman
Mickey Gomez	Jerry O'Hare	Claire Axelrad

Jason Shim	Mary Cahalane	Ephraim Gopin
Thomas Negron	Nancy Schwartz	Darian R. Heyman
Beth Locke	Lori Jacobwith	Marc Pitman
Hildy Gottlieb	Estrella Moser	Ash Shepherd
Amy Sample Ward	Danielle Brigida	Sam Rubin
Aimee Vance	John Lepp	Phil Gerbyshak
Mark Horvath	Emily Rubin	Jay Wilkinson
Rachel Muir	Randy Hawthorne	Vanessa Chase
Matt Rubin	Peter Drury	Chris Tuttle
Jules Rubin	Julia Campbell	Noland Hoshino
Michelle Brinson	Sharon G. Macken	Farra Trompeter
Eve Simon	Antionette Kerr	Seth Peterson
Tammy Zonker	Shonali Burke	Sandy Rees
Rachel Lee Bearbower	Norman Reiss	Carrie Rice
Steve Chaggaris	Danny Brown	Janet Fout
Bob Mastroianni	BenBen Jam	
Suzanne Wiezbicki	Ronni Gentile	

To you all, this book is a reply to your ingenuity and dedication to leaving a positive dent in this world.

Thank you, thank you, thank you! I totally owe you!

Part One

WHY CARE?

Introduction

There's a Seinfeld episode where Jerry and Elaine make a reservation for a rental car, only to be told by the agent that the company has run out of cars. It goes something like this:

Jerry: Do you have my reservation?

Car rental agent: Yes, we do. Unfortunately, we ran out of cars.

Jerry: But the reservation keeps the car here. That's why you have the reservation.

Car rental agent: I know why we have reservations.

Jerry: I don't think you do. If you did, I'd have a car . . .

Car rental agent: Let me speak, uh, with my supervisor . . .

Car rental agent: I'm sorry, my supervisor said there's nothing we can do, but we do have a compact . . . A blue Ford Escort. Would you like insurance?

Jerry: Yes, you better give me the insurance, because I'm gonna beat the hell out of this car.

If you laughed, it's because you can relate to Jerry's exasperation and his desire for sweet, sweet revenge. However, laughter and fantasies of justice won't take away the wasted time, money, and frustration we've all experienced from lousy customer service. We remember bad customer service, sometimes for years, much more than we remember excellent customer service.

Bad customer service doesn't only impact most consumers. It affects the organizations that, knowingly or unknowingly, don't care for their customers as much as they should. In fact, lousy customer service costs businesses in the United States over $75 billion a year, according to a report published in *Forbes* Magazine.

The report shared that because "brands are failing to create the positive, emotional experiences that drive customer loyalty," 67 percent of customers are "serial switchers," switching brands at the drop of a hat because of poor customer service.

To make matters even worse, these "serial switchers," after having bad customer service, tell an average of seven friends about that bad experience.

If you think that this phenomenon doesn't occur in the nonprofit sector, you are woefully wrong, or just aren't being honest about the possible lack of care that exists in your organization. Yes, it hurts to look at our mistakes. However, seeing them, with courage, is always the first step to change.

Here is what a few of my friends said on Twitter about their recent bad experiences with nonprofits:

"For a year and a half—NOTHING. Maybe an email thank you. Never a word about what my gift was accomplishing. Never a thank-you letter."—@PamelaGrow

"I made a memorial gift to a suicide prevention org. I was charged, but I never received an acknowledgment. Multiple attempts to contact them via email and phone were ignored. I have no idea if the memorial acknowledgment was sent."—@ThomasNegron

"I made a first-time donation to an org last week, received a transaction receipt and then got a fundraising ask five hours after my first donation."—@vanessaechase

"I was never a donor, but I'm constantly thanked for my support, asked for my continued support, told the results of my support?? Not only does it make me angry as a fundraiser, it pisses me off as a person that an org cares so little to take the time to do it rt."—@DJVermenton

"I gave a fairly large, unsolicited donation to a very small, under-funded nonprofit about three weeks ago. I had hoped it would be received with delight, but so far I've heard crickets. Leaves me with the feeling that I've done the wrong thing."—@thewhinydonor

In Part One, let's look at what bad customer service and communications in the nonprofit sector have created. Then we'll talk about how to not only overcome these poor results but to use real, human CARE—connecting, appreciating, replying, and encouraging—to do more than you ever thought possible for your fundraising and your mission.

CHAPTER 1

Why Donor Retention is Essential

I have been studying donor retention rates in the nonprofit sector for over ten years and they are consistently dismal. Donor retention rates have been below 50 percent since tracked by the Fundraising Effectiveness Project. Nonprofits as a whole are losing more donors than they are keeping. Essentially, they are bleeding to death.

Donor retention is a measure of how many donors give to an organization year after year. Sadly, too many nonprofits don't know their retention rates. Interestingly, however, nonprofits that begin tracking retention rates generally see an improvement. This is likely because tracking donor retention indicates that an organization is serious about donor care.

Let's peel back donor retention for first-time, repeat, and monthly donors.

First-time donors are people who gave to an organization for the very first time. According to the Fundraising Effectiveness

Project, 2018 retention rates for first-time donors are only 29 percent. That means 71 percent of the first-time donors never come back to make a second gift. Many times this is because a first-time gift is impulsive, or given in response to a disaster, like Hurricane Harvey, which netted a windfall of over $1 billion in donations during the months that followed.

Repeat donors are people who gave again after the first gift. At 49 percent, retention rates for repeat donors are much better than first-time donors. People who give twice to an organization are more committed than people who only give once, such as impulsive givers and disaster givers.

Monthly donors are people who give via credit card or checking account automatically each month. DonorPerfect reports that their nonprofit clients have seen a retention rate of 90 percent or more among monthly donors. A monthly giving program can more than double your donor retention rates!

The High Costs of Donor Attrition

Because most nonprofits aren't tracking their donor retention rates (less than 50 percent do according to the Fundraising Effectiveness Project), they're unaware of the hidden costs of high attrition. Not tracking donor retention usually signals that the organization is short-sighted in its goals, living hand-to-mouth in its fundraising.

Caring for donors after the first gift impacts revenue in three powerful ways:

- It reduces the costs of acquisition, which can be as high as ten times the cost of retention.

- It increases the lifetime value of donors. Donors who feel loved are loyal. So donor loyalty has a compounding effect.
- It reduces the cost of other efforts that impact loyalty. Loyal donors also make for loyal volunteers, advocates, peer-to-peer fundraisers, etc.

At the end of this chapter, we'll look at how to calculate your retention rates for your organization.

For now, let's dig further into each of these benefits of caring for donors after their first gift.

High Donor Retention Reduces Your Fundraising Costs

Acquiring a new donor is not cheap. Creating awareness for your nonprofit, encouraging donors to decide if your nonprofit is worthy, and finally encouraging donors to give all cost money. Direct mail campaigns might seem like one of the highest costs, but don't forget about staff salaries, developing your brand, maintaining your website, software, marketing and fundraising consulting, telemarketing, advertising, etc. For nonprofits that raise most of their money from fundraising events, these costs can be even higher. If you take all of these costs and divide them by the number of donors acquired from these efforts, you might be shocked.

On average, the first gift from a new donor rarely covers the cost of acquiring that donor. In *Building Donor Loyalty: The Fundraiser's Guide to Increasing Lifetime Value*, Adrian Sargeant and Elaine Jay say that the cost of acquiring a new donor can be as much as ten times the cost of retaining a donor.

But current donors who have already demonstrated that they like, know, and trust you—proven by the fact that they've given you money—cost much less to retain. Why? Because they are already aware of your cause and they've decided that, of all the nonprofits out there, yours is most deserving of their hard-earned money.

Creating awareness and motivating decisions are the most costly aspects of marketing. But keeping donors happy—caring for them—is up to 10 times cheaper than replacing them. This is simply because current donors have already demonstrated a very conspicuous commitment to your organization.

Another Wonder of the World: The Compounding Effect of Lifetime Donor Value

Any veteran fundraiser will agree that the real value of a donor is not in the first gift; it's in the accumulation of gifts they give to the organization throughout the relationship, which can last for years. Once a donor gives three or four times, they will most likely stick around for at least a few years. On the flip-side, because high attrition rates equal a lower lifetime value for donors, this can negatively impact future revenue for nonprofits to the tune of millions of dollars.

In *Building Donor Loyalty*, Adrian Sergeant and Elaine Jay present the following example of two organizations, both of which started with $5 million in donations. The first organization has a 10 percent attrition rate and ends up with $33 million in 10 years. The second organization has a 20 percent attrition rate and ends up with $22 million in 10 years. Both organizations are exactly the same, meaning that they have the same number of donors giving the same amounts each year. But the second organization loses more donors each year than the first organization. Summarizing this example, the authors write, "In other words, the impact of cutting the attrition rate from 20 percent to 10 percent will have equated in an improvement in profitability of 50 percent."

The Value of Loyal Donors Goes Way Beyond Money

Loyal donors are much more likely to be volunteers, fundraisers, and advocates. Again, they don't narrowly define and segment how they give.

Loyal donors will often make additional gifts in response to special appeals. They'll also be more likely to volunteer, lowering the costs for volunteer acquisition. Loyal donors will also more likely become peer-to-peer fundraisers, recruiting their friends to give to the organization.

Lastly, loyal donors share excellent testimonials and will definitely bring many new donors to the organization through word-of-mouth marketing.

Loyal Donors Fuel Your Mission

It goes without saying that your nonprofit cannot accomplish its mission without being sustainable.

Sustainability is about vision and leadership, but it's also about funding. Your nonprofit will cease to exist without funds, and if your funding source is mostly derived from donors, then sustainability means growing a loyal base of donors.

Sustainability is also about predicting the future. In terms of fundraising, this means being able to predict how much revenue will be coming in the door next year, in five years, and so on.

One powerful way to create financial predictability is with an automated monthly giving program.

Because monthly giving automatically charges a donor each month, it allows you to plan ahead. Monthly donors agree, in advance, to pay you each month. This agreement and the automation allow you to predict, down to the penny, how much funding your nonprofit can depend upon at any point in the future.

We Have Conditioned Donors to Expect Less, and That's a Problem

When nonprofits don't care about their donors, the entire sector feels the impact, not just the one organization. Because high attrition is essentially a chronic epidemic that has lasted for decades, donors have stopped expecting more. An informal poll of my friends found that they expect more from retailers and for-profits than they do from nonprofits.

A dear friend and colleague expressed this lowering of the bar by saying, "They're busy doing good for society, so it's okay that they don't have the resources to do good for their donors." No, it's not okay in my book, and it shouldn't be in yours either, for all the reasons mentioned in this chapter.

How to Calculate Your Nonprofit's Donor Retention Rates

Are you ready to improve your donor retention rates? It starts with knowing what your numbers are. Here's how to find them.

1. Gather Your Data

To calculate your retention rates, you will need to gather two types of data:

- Data about your donors, such as donor ID and donor name.

- Data about their gifts, such as giving dates and amounts for the past several years.

2. Calculate Year-over-Year Retention

Of the donors who gave in a given year (let's call it year one), how many gave again the following year (let's call that year two)?

Count the total number of donors who gave in year one. Note, this not just first-time donors, but all donors who gave in that year.

Count the total number of donors who gave in year two.

Divide the number of donors in year two by the donors in year one and then multiply by 100.

For example, if 1,000 donors gave in year 1 and 500 donors returned to give again in year 2, you retained 50 percent of your donors and lost 50 percent of your donors.

3. Look at Multiple Years

Of course, donors are not robots, so many cannot give year after year. Sometimes they lose their jobs or have some other reason why they might skip a year or more. For this reason, it's good to see retention from the perspective of multiple years. It's common that a donor who gave to you five years ago suddenly again shows up to make another gift. The fact that they showed up again signals their loyalty.

4. Start Tracking These Retention Metrics

First-time Donor Retention. The percentage of first-time donors giving a second gift.

Returning Donor Retention. The percentage of donors giving two or more gifts that give again.

Average Annual Gift. The total annual gifts in dollars is divided by the total number of donors. Changes in average annual gift amounts, especially if they're shrinking, could mean that you need to develop strategies to increase gift amounts.

Lifetime Value. The amount an organization can expect from the average donor over the lifetime of the relationship.

Donor Acquisition Costs. The cost incurred by an organization to recruit someone to make a donation.

5. Don't Compare Your Nonprofit to Other Organizations

Comparing your data to peer organizations is fruitless. Doing so will either make you feel bad (if your current situation is worse) or become complacent (if your retention rates are higher). The only thing you have control over is your organization and how you treat your donors. Focus on that.

With your data in hand, let's look at your communications.

CHAPTER 2

CAREless Donor Communications

Nonprofit leaders have failed. A culture of arrogance and carelessness permeates executive offices and boardrooms everywhere. Puffed up with conceit, many leaders focus on their organization's achievements. They take credit for all of the nonprofit's successes, acknowledging donors as mere footnotes, as if they were ATMs.

As a result of myopic attitude, nonprofits struggle to keep donors. Donors come, they give, and they don't return. Nonprofits miss the connection between making the donor feel important and the impact on fundraising results. It's carelessness on behalf of the nonprofit.

Nonprofits love the thrill of the new donor. Many organizations focus on acquisition without putting any effort into nurturing the relationship. It's like when a couple starts dating. Everything is new and filled with excitement. But the freshness wanes as time passes. To keep the relationship healthy and strong, you have to work at it every day, or it will fail.

CAREless donor communications equates to disconnection, lack of appreciation, unresponsiveness, and discouragement. These four sins are the ultimate cause for poor donor loyalty, starting from inside the hearts of leaders at the top of the organization, all the way down to donor appeals and thank-you notes (if any exist at all).

CARElessness is a systemic problem, not a tactical one.

The same is true with your donor relationships. You work hard to bring in new donors. New donors take time and money to acquire. So when a donor makes a first gift, you cannot assume you've sealed the deal. You cannot treat the relationship like a transaction. After all, the first gift is a test. It's a test to find out how much you value the donor and their part in making a meaningful impact.

And treating donors badly has consequences. You pay a price when you have a culture of arrogance and carelessness. That enormous cost is poor donor retention, which leads to declining fundraising revenue.

But you are different. You have the power to change all of this! You see all of this as an opportunity to significantly improve how you communicate with donors—especially after that first gift. You picture the potential, and you recognize that only you can fill the gaps in your donor communications. I can just hear the bells going off in that amazing brain of yours!

Now, if you've looked around at peer organizations, you'll notice that most are not caring for their donors in even the most basic ways. Let's look at what's happening.

Failure to Launch

In 2015, GiveCentral conducted a survey called *Predictions for Nonprofit Giving* and it highlighted just how nonprofits are missing the mark.

Although 84 percent of participating organizations claimed to embrace technology, more than 27 percent don't consistently communicate with donors with email. And only 10 percent communicate with donors every week. Clearly, this is a failure to launch—to leverage even basic strategies to keep donors happy.

A deeper dive into the survey reveals that

- 27 percent of nonprofits lack a schedule for emails
- 54 percent lack a schedule for phone calls
- 89 percent have no plan for text messaging
- 78 percent email donors less than once a month
- 90 percent email donors less than once a week

But lacking a communications schedule is just one symptom of a bigger problem: lacking a donor communications strategy.

In my own professional experience, working with hundreds of nonprofits over the past decade, most nonprofits aren't caring for their donors in the most basic ways:

- Most nonprofits barely send a thank-you note to new donors. Even if they do, it's rarely a memorable experience for donors.
- Most nonprofits don't send handwritten thank-you notes to new donors. Many view it as a costly obligation.
- Most nonprofits don't ask new donors why they gave ... even though we know surveying donors makes them more likely to give again.

- Most nonprofits fail to report back to donors about the impact of the gift.
- Most nonprofits fail to report back about the people benefiting from a donor's gift.
- Most nonprofits fail to ask first-time donors for a second gift.
- Most nonprofits fail to invite new donors to join a monthly giving program.
- Most nonprofits don't have a stewardship plan for new donors.
- Most nonprofits aren't using technology to automate and scale effective donor communications.
- Most nonprofits aren't personalizing their communications to first-time donors.

If you aren't doing most of the strategies mentioned above, it means that your donors probably aren't loyal. They simply aren't having experiences with your organization that makes them feel appreciated and that makes them feel like they matter.

They don't feel cared for.

Unhappy Donors Don't Keep It to Themselves

When a donor leaves because they're unhappy, you don't just lose the one person. According to Adrian Sargeant's *Building Donor Loyalty*, "Dissatisfied donors tell about seven of their friends or relatives about the experience they had, and thus they can seriously damage the nonprofit's image and standing in the local or national community."

If you lost 100 donors last year, you really lost 700. It's just like that shampoo commercial, but instead of telling two friends about their new shimmer, they tell seven not to give to your nonprofit!

Should I Stay or Should I Go Now?

You're welcome for the Clash earworm.

There are four essential questions that every donor always asks:

1. Why give?

2. Why me?

3. Why now?

4. Did my gift matter?

I'll cut to the chase: Donors leave because the nonprofit didn't care if they stayed. And caring is well within an organization's control. Again, it's a failure to launch—a failure to communicate effectively with donors after they make a donation.

A study from Indiana University, in partnership with Bloomerang and the Center for Philanthropy, found that over 84 percent of the reasons that donors leave can be fixed with better donor communications. Here's what donors said and how communications could have helped.

- 5 percent—Said the charity didn't need them. *Donors won't keep giving if you don't tell them they matter.*
- 8 percent—Said they did not receive information on how the donations were used. *This is a guaranteed way NOT to get a second gift.*
- 9 percent—Said they had no memory of supporting the charity. *No memory? Wow, this is really the lowest bar.*
- 13 percent—Said they never got thanked for donating. *Adequately thanking donors increases retention rates and lifetime value.*

- 18 percent—Said they received poor service or communications. *They are telling you directly they want better communications.*
- 36 percent—Said others were more deserving. *Organizations that don't communicate a clear case for support are vulnerable to competition.*
- 54 percent—Said they could no longer afford to give. *In this case, it's not that donors aren't supporting any cause, just not yours.*

Why Donors Stay

Roger Craver, one of the geniuses behind *The Agitator* and author of *Retention Fundraising: The New Art and Science of Keeping Your Donors for Life*, outlines seven factors that cause donors to stick around.

1. She perceives your organization is effective in achieving its mission.
2. She knows what to expect from your organization with each interaction.
3. She receives a timely thank you.
4. She has opportunities to make her views known.
5. She feels she is part of an important cause.
6. She feels her involvement is appreciated.
7. She receives information showing who is being helped.

Understanding why donors stick around and why donors leave is vital. More specifically, understanding why YOUR donors stay or go is the first best step to fixing the problem.

Once you understand the "why" for your organization, your path will be clear. And with the tactics outlined in this book, you'll be able to fix the leaks that might exist in your own donor communications plan.

See for Yourself

Here's a pro tip for you: Make a small donation to five nonprofits who are your best competition. Pick nonprofits that do similar work in the eyes of your donors (solve homelessness, find homes for dogs, fight cancer, etc.).

Review how your donor experience compares for each nonprofit. Then ask yourself:

- How are you telling donors their gift makes a difference?
- How can you be better about reporting outcomes?
- How can you be better at on-boarding new donors?
- How can you be better at dazzling your donors?

Now that you have a better understanding of why your donors might stop giving, you can work to ensure that they stay. It all starts with CAREful donor communications.

CHAPTER 3

CAREful Donor Communications

The value of great donor communications has already been researched and proven and many nonprofits are trying to put it into practice. Great fundraising minds like Tom Ahern, Adrian Sargeant, Kivi Leroux Miller, Jeff Brooks, and Harvey McKinnon have all written books on effective donor communications.

This book focuses on one thing: How to use marketing and effective communications to build donor loyalty **after** the first gift. If you're looking for ways to acquire new donors, this is not the book. If you're looking for ways to keep donors coming back, read on.

What is Good Donor Communications?

Is there really a difference between good fundraising communications and excellent relationship building? Both involve connecting, appreciating, replying, and encouraging.

Reread those words. Notice the letter that each word begins with: It creates the word CARE!

Remarkable fundraising is about great human relationships that are based on care. But how do we extend that to our marketing? How do we automate it? How do we systematize it? This is where a simple framework becomes useful.

So what is this "CAREful" donor communications that I speak of? Let's dive in.

The Donor CARE Framework: A Simple Recipe

I've developed a simple recipe for you to remember. I call it Donor CARE.

C = Connect

A = Appreciate

R = Reply

E = Encourage

The one thing that ties the CARE framework together is that the ingredients are all human qualities. All people want to connect, be appreciated, feel heard, and be encouraged.

Let's look a little closer.

Connect

To connect is human. When we feel connected, we feel recognized as an individual. We feel valued for our uniqueness. We feel valued for our story.

Good fundraising connects. It connects donors with their stories. It connects donors with their community. It connects donors with resources. It connects donors with the impact that they have made.

Donors want to know that their support makes a difference. That makes sense, doesn't it? According to Bloomerang, 5 percent of donors leave because they think the nonprofit doesn't need them.

Appreciate

To appreciate means more than just to value. I appreciate YOU. When I say this I mean yes, I do value you. But I also increase your value to both of us. That's the incredible thing about appreciation. It impacts both the giver and receiver. When you say thank you, you are suddenly focused on the other. You've become bigger. When someone thanks you, you feel like your efforts matter, that you matter.

Appreciation also makes your brand bigger. Nonprofit brands that show appreciation regularly, like Alex's Lemonade Stand Foundation, are bigger precisely because they appreciate their donors. When they brag about one of their donors, they're bragging about ALL of their donors.

Appreciation also raises more money, as you shall see. But appreciation has to be more than obligatory or grudging. Appreciation has to be sincere in order to be felt the way that it needs to be felt.

"Thank you" expresses what it means to be human, what it means to be interconnected with others. "Thank you" calls forth the power of gratitude within your life.

Reply

Good communications between human beings is a back-and-forth. We learned this in middle school when we studied the basic model of communication: Sender, receiver, message, feedback, repeat.

When we reply, we let the other person know that they were heard. We validate their story, their concerns, and their experience.

I'll be honest: It was difficult for me to settle on a single word for this aspect of the CARE model. Throughout writing this book, I jumped back and forth between *reply, respond,* and *report back*. For our purposes, *reply* will include all of that.

Replying deepens our relationships. If you've ever had a penpal, you'd agree. If you grew up with texting or even video games as a way to connect with friends, no doubt the best friends were the ones who responded to your messages and gave you feedback on your bad shooter skills.

Replying is also critical to developing relationships with donors. And I'm not talking about the reply envelope in your annual appeal. I'm talking about responding to donors when they have questions. Responding quickly. Surveying donors is also a way to reply. And the research shows that when donors feel they have an opportunity to make their views known, they are more likely to stick around and give more.

As time goes on, donors will naturally forget about your nonprofit—unless you stay in touch!

It's not enough to simply have a single autoresponder that thanks people every time they make a donation. Each donor at each level of giving should receive regular communications reminding them of the great work you're doing, and how they played a central role in it.

Encourage

You and your donors are on a journey together. And it naturally starts after the first gift where they encouraged you, and you encouraged them.

When donors give to your organization for the very first time, their expectations are wide open. How you treat them immediately after that gift sets the tone for the relationship. Are you treating that relationship as if you were sending them down a dead-end? Or are you on a journey together, encouraging each other to create a better world that you both envision?

Encourage donors to take that next step, whether it's sharing your Giving Tuesday fundraiser that they just gave to, following you on Instagram, inviting their friends to donate to a Facebook fundraiser, or joining your monthly giving program.

Now that you know what CARE is, let's go deeper into its true power to change your nonprofit, and therefore unleash goodness into the world. But first I'd like to share a story about my heart to illustrate how "care" manifests between people.

CHAPTER 4

The Flow and Dynamism of CARE

What Color is Care? How Much Does It Weigh?

My heart was literally being crushed. Literally.

Early one morning in late March, 2018, I awoke from a nightmare sweating and felt my heart fluttering. Ba boom, ba boom, and the pause. Boom boom boom, another pause. After speaking to my oncologist who was on call, we raced to the emergency room.

The doctors quickly determined that I wasn't having a heart attack. Instead, there was something else wrong with my heart. I was scheduled for an EKG and an echocardiogram. The results showed I had what's called a pericardial effusion. There was over a cup of fluid between my pericardium and my heart.

Imagine your heart is a balloon. And that balloon is surrounded by another balloon. Normally, a little fluid is in between the two to provide lubricant. But because of the inflammation in my surrounding organs caused by the tumor in my chest, fluid was building up around my heart. And that fluid was literally crushing my heart.

To remove the fluid, the cardiologist, a young man who didn't look a day over 30, would insert a catheter in my chest, sneaking around my heart, to allow the fluid to drain through the catheter over the next two days.

I asked the cardiologist, who actually had a very dry sense of humor, "So doc, how do you remove the catheter? Do you just pull it out like zip, zip?"

Without batting an eye, he replied "Yes." I thought he was kidding, but he was absolutely serious.

He reassured me that the procedure of putting in the catheter would be painless since I would be under conscious sedation. I asked him about removing the catheter, and he said that there would be no need for anesthesia. They would simply pull it out like a ripcord. He said it would be a little uncomfortable, but it wouldn't hurt a bit.

Two days later, with the fluid now gone, I was told that my cardiologist would remove the catheter sometime that evening. I went about my business of doing pretty much nothing, as one does when they stay in the hospital. While hopped up on prednisone, I kept myself busy reading, chanting, and finding myself strangely memorized by *Days of Our Lives.*

At exactly 7:00 p.m., a young man poked his head in my room to introduce himself. "I'm Kevin, I'll be your nurse tonight." I was like, "OK, a male nurse, that's cool." The nurses I'd seen that week had all been women, so a male nurse was a little bit of a surprise—but not the biggest surprise I had that week.

Fifteen minutes later, my cardiologist and Kevin entered my room. "Ready?" he asked as Kevin snapped on a pair of purple hospital gloves. "Right now, right here?" I started freaking out inside. I wasn't ready.

I quickly determined that my only choice was to somehow tell Kevin that I was feeling really vulnerable. "Kevin, I'm feeling a little nervous about this. I don't even like the sight of my own blood. I'm kind of freaking out inside," I said.

Kevin completely reassured me. He told me that it was OK for me to be scared and that he would be right there with me. He said I could look away and he would describe exactly what the doctor was doing as he was doing it. He put his arm around me and held me in the hospital bed. He completely embraced me in my total state of vulnerability.

"OK, the doctor is now removing the bandage. Now he is sterilizing the site." After a few minutes, the doctor said, "OK, we're going to count to three together and pull the catheter out. Ready?"

I had no choice but to completely let go and let Kevin care for me. Together Kevin and my cardiologist counted, "One, two, three" and I felt a strange sensation as the cardiologist quickly pulled the catheter out of my chest. Zip! Just like that.

You can imagine how relieved I was to have the procedure over. I commented on how amazing it was. It really was painless, and Kevin made it so easy for me because he truly cared. He embraced me in his care and I received his care with my decided vulnerability.

Where Does Care Exist?

In my moment of vulnerability that evening, I thought about care. Kevin cared for me, and I allowed him to care for me. But where did that care exist? Would it have existed if Kevin had no one to care for? And would I have felt that care if someone wasn't caring for me?

Does care exist separately from the hearts and minds of those who are giving and receiving care? Does care exist anywhere outside you and me?

That night, Kevin changed the way I viewed donor care, forever.

I believe—and I'm sure you do too—that care truly manifests between two or more people. Although one can care for themselves (and we'll look at self-care later in this book), CARE can only exist in relationships with others. We don't live in isolation. We are all cells, each a unique, infinitely important part of the massive beautiful organism we call life. And at work you play an equally important role as a cell in the organism that is your nonprofit.

Care only exists in the hearts of people in relationships with each other. Even when we think about others, like dear friends, or loved ones, and we feel care towards them, that is only because there is a relationship.

This is my conclusion after thinking about the essence of care for many years, as a Buddhist, as a parent, a friend, and yes, as a marketing consultant for nonprofits.

What Does It Really Mean for Nonprofits to Care?

Nonprofits often talk about caring for donors. But what does it mean to really care for donors?

Does that care exist in the emails we send? Does that care exist in the direct mail pieces, the Facebook ads, etc.?

Yes and no.

Things can't care—only people can. Things like email, social media, or website copy can only convey care that exists between people.

We see lots of donor communications where the care is missing.

If the people, particularly the leadership within an organization, harbor a sense of arrogance towards donors in their hearts, viewing donors as inferior to themselves, the donors will feel it. Even if the organization hires the best copywriter who pours heart and soul into writing a sincere appeal letter, chances are the leadership won't have the courage to send it.

If nonprofit leadership harbors a sense of arrogance and superiority, it probably already has policies in place to review every piece of communications that goes out the door. Once that beautifully written appeal letter gets reviewed by the leaders, they, no doubt, will remove any heart it had in it. "We would never say these things to our donors," was what one nonprofit leader said to me.

Obviously, the above example is pretty extreme and, admittedly, negative. But the point is that the state of the hearts and minds of leadership in your organization has the greatest role in nurturing donor loyalty. Leadership has the most influence on creating a culture of care that includes happy employees and care-centered policies and processes.

Low retention rates can ultimately be tied back to the attitude of leadership in an organization. Conversely, high retention rates are often an obvious reflection of the culture within an organization—built with a caring heart by leaders who get it.

The Immeasurable Can Still be Managed

The state of care within an individual's heart can't possibly be quantified. It can't be measured. There is limitless potential in each person for appreciation and willingness to connect, willingness to dialogue, and capacity to encourage. These qualities cannot be measured, but their proxies can. Proxies for care include things like email open rates, repeat website visitors, donor surveys, etc.

And there's one big proxy: donor loyalty. The change within the hearts and minds of people within an organization who embrace CARE will always be reflected in donor loyalty.

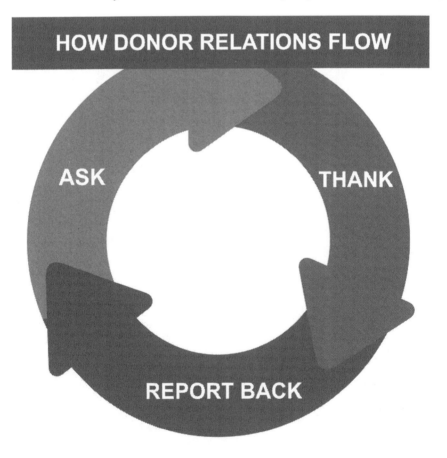

If you look at each element of CARE, you might begin to see something familiar: The flow or rhythm of donor stewardship.

The top experts in the field of fundraising agree with a general cycle of giving that goes like this:

- Thank
- Report back
- Ask

CARE overlays and supports the cycle of giving:

- CONNECT—Before an ask even happens, a connection must be made.
- APPRECIATE—Thank
- REPLY—Report back
- ENCOURAGE—Ask

Because YOU are infinitely dynamic, so is CARE.

There's a Buddhist concept revealed in the Lotus Sutra called the mutual possessions of the 10 worlds. It's a classification of ten states of life that expresses the dynamism that exists within each human life. Briefly, the ten worlds ranging from hell all the way to Buddhahood:

- Buddhahood
- Bodhisattva
- Realization
- Learning
- Rapture
- Tranquility
- Anger
- Animality

- Hunger
- Hell

Regardless of what religion or spirituality you follow, we've all had the experience of hearing the front door ring only to be delivered a large unexpected bill, or possibly a court summons. At that moment, we drop to the world of hell. We are at the mercy of our environment. We are shaken.

Another common experience we've all had is meeting that special someone, going out on a few dates, and then realizing they're not as perfect as we initially thought. This initial stage of Rapture often leads to a trap tour of Hell (hopelessness), and sometimes even Anger if the person wasn't honest about who they were. It's a big let down. We've all had these experiences.

Many times, these experiences motivate us to go deeper with our lives so that we stop repeating the same pattern. Eventually, we are unswayed when a bill collector shows up at our door, or when our brand-new soulmate suddenly stops returning our calls.

The ideal of the mutual possession of the ten worlds means that each of the ten worlds contains the other.

For example, if you were delivered a court summons by a sheriff at your front door (hopefully this never happens to you), this could possibly motivate you to eventually take responsibility for the situation because you REALIZE that it's wiser to set up a payment plan for your debt, instead of running away from the problem. So the world of Realization is contained within the world of Hell. Of course, it's up to you to make the change.

You can learn more about the ten worlds and Buddhism by Googling it, but for now I'm stealing this concept to discuss the mutual possession of CARE. In other words, each element of CARE must contain all three other elements to be truly effective.

For example, to effectively appreciate your donor, you must also connect with them (make sure they're the right contact in your database, understand their relationship with your organization), be willing to dialogue and respond to them (reply), and approach them with an encouraging, positive tone.

If one element is missing, then it won't be as impactful as you'd like. For example, an appreciative thank-you note with a tone of discouragement is obviously not appreciation but some sort of passive-aggressive fundraising strategy. Take "Thank you for your generous gift of $10. It'll go a long way to feed the homeless in Chicago." This could be read as being very sarcastic and demoralizing.

A Checklist for the Mutual Possession of CARE

Let's dive in a little bit deeper about how you can apply the mutual possession of care within your retention strategy. Think of this approach like a simple checklist, making sure that each care element contains at least some of the three other elements.

For example, let's say you are sending a welcome email filled with appreciation. Make sure that email is sent to the right people at the right time in your database (connect), that you are willing and able to reply to emails (because many will reply to your email), and that your email contains some element of encouragement, for example, a next step. Something like this embodies the four elements: "Thank you for your donation. You made a big difference in someone's life. Please join our community of people just like you on Facebook."

The 8 Laws of CARE

John Lennon's "Imagine" is a song about removing barriers and revealing the oneness of all people.

Buddhism talks of being "one with everything." And whether we are Buddhists or not, we all would like to agree that we're all connected in a big story called humanity. Regardless of religion, I think most people would agree that adopting a mindset of oneness or being connected to all is a good thing.

In fact, quantum science and quantum theory are on the cutting edge of validating what the Buddha said almost 3,000 years ago. A oneness exists between each person, other people, and the environment.

We experience this oneness every single day. To me, it's pretty obvious. In those moments when I'm feeling worthless, arrogant, begrudging, cheerless, or angry, it's always reflected in my environment, specifically, the people around me at that moment!

Whenever Kate asks me to do the dishes and I complain, it never ends up going in a positive direction. I've learned to just do the dishes. But if I can wash those dishes to my best ability, cheerfully and with a sense of humor, then that's all for the better, and one step closer to world peace in the household.

The same is true at work. You're a human being at home and you're a human being at work. It's not like you go to work and suddenly you're not a human. Therefore, the law of oneness and environment applies every day and at your job too.

If the Buddha were a fundraiser and wanted to increase donor loyalty, this might be the Buddha's checklist:

❑ Fundraisers and donors are equal in their worthiness and value. Both share the unlimited capacity to CARE.

❑ Separateness (us/them) is an illusion.

❑ The collective feelings of worthlessness, arrogance, complaint, and anger will always cause poor donor loyalty.

❑ The collective feelings of worthiness, connectedness, appreciation, and positivity will always cause an increase in donor loyalty.

❑ Every individual in an organization can change.

❑ Every individual in an organization has the power to affect change.

❑ If employees are unhappy, donors will leave.

❑ If employees are happy, donors will stay.

CHAPTER 5

The Competitive Edge of CARE

At this point, it's probably clear that even something as simple as thanking your donors can make your nonprofit stand apart from the competition. Very few nonprofits are doing even the basics of good donor communications. Again, many nonprofits don't even track their retention rates, much less do anything about it.

"It's lonely at the top. Ninety-nine percent of people in the world are convinced they are incapable of achieving great things, so they aim for the mediocre. The level of competition is thus fiercest for 'realistic' goals, paradoxically making them the most time and energy-consuming."—Tim Ferriss

What Tim says is also true for organizations, since they're the sum of the people who run them. Too many nonprofits aim to be mediocre, to be average—whether because of following "best practices" that too many others are following, having your brilliant ideas shot down by the committee, or fear that you'll offend someone or rock the boat. Again, too many nonprofits aim to be average.

Many don't even have a written marketing plan. After a few failed starts, expectations are lowered. They give up, not because they lack will power or passion but because they lack planning and training.

After a while, they start thinking that they'll never raise enough money, never wow donors, never actually really achieve the lofty mission they were once so excited about. So why even try? If this sounds mean, it's not. It's just true.

The truth is, most of the nonprofits you compete with don't *want* to stand out. They want to play it safe, to be invisible. They're sheep.

But you? You're the wolf!

The first thing I recommend to nonprofit newbies at an organization is that they subscribe and donate to their closest competition. This sort of easy research allows you to identify areas of weakness where you can stand apart quickly. It also enables you to get ideas about things they're doing right and best practices for your own use.

So, will you be part of the 99 percent, the vanilla? Or will you be the 1 percent, the double chocolate espresso? Will you be the nonprofit that stands out by creating experiences donors won't soon forget?

Become the Purple Cow of Causes in Your Sector

Purple Cow: Transform Your Business by Being Remarkable is a book by Seth Godin. It changed how I view marketing, and it will change how you think about marketing and how attention works.

At the beginning of the book, Seth shares a story about a road trip he took with his family to the country. Being a family from the city, Seth's kids had only seen cows on TV. As they drove further away from the city, there they were: "Cows!" the kids cried. "Mommy, daddy, look at them!"

As they continued to drive past dairy farms, they saw more cows. They saw brown cows, black-and-white cows, big fat cows, and baby cows. Eventually, the cows weren't that remarkable anymore. They drove on, and on, past more and more cows. Until suddenly, they saw something they had never seen before. "Mommy, daddy—look—a purple cow!" They were just as excited as when they saw the very first cow at the beginning of their road trip.

Now, whether there was actually a purple cow or not is not the point of the story. The story is about how attention works. Your goal is to be the purple cow in your donors' mind—to stand out among the field of cows that donors have become bored with.

Seth promoted the *Purple Cow* using many of the techniques that Godin describes in his book, packaging it in a milk carton. The cover is purple and white, and the words were printed sideways.

"Today, the one sure way to fail is to be boring. Your one chance for success is to be remarkable."—Seth Godin

What does this mean for you? When your competition goes left, you go right. Create contrast. Create donor experiences that are remarkable . . . experiences they'll tell their friends about! Of course, you can extend Purple Cow thinking throughout your entire organization, to every way that you operate, from your services and your online experiences to your brand and differentiation.

However, we are here to talk about building donor loyalty. Your goal is to create remarkable donor experiences for your donors.

What Does Your Nonprofit Really Sell

Money for nothing? When donors give you money, they get nothing in return. Or do they?

My son's sneakers used to be cheap, even with the blinking lights. He loved the blinking lights. And the Lighting McQueen racing stripes. They never failed to put a big smile on his face and make me feel like the worlds #1 dad.

Then my son became a teenager. He wanted the newest Air Jordan Nikes for $180—$180 for a pair of sneakers? What happened to Keds? What happened to cheap Converse? Note: $180 is nothing compared to the Nike Foamposite One "Sole Collector" that retailed for $6,000 in 1997.

The only way I'd get $180 worth of value was to make this purchase a teachable moment. The lesson? Understanding that the high price had everything to do with how he hoped the sneakers would make him feel about himself.

Our deal: I'd pay for the sneakers if he'd pay for the feeling. He's paying for the story.

What are Stories Worth?

You've probably heard a board member say something that follows seemingly logical reasoning. Or maybe you yourself have thought this:

"Our donors are really smart. They don't like to be manipulated."

"Why can't they just donate to help us lower the percent of at-risk youth who re-offend and reenter the prison system? Aren't statistics compelling enough?"

"Clearly we've demonstrated how our water filters work. Have you seen the before and after pics? They're very reliable and easy to use."

What value do stories really add to your fundraising strategy? Rob Walker and Joshua Glenn had a similar question and used eBay to get an answer. Their project, *Significant Objects,* sought to answer a simple question: Is it possible to place an objective value on stories?

The project auctioned off thrift-store objects via eBay, each one including a short story about the object written by one of over 200 contributing writers. The objects, purchased for $250, sold for nearly $8,000 in total. (Proceeds were distributed to the contributors and to nonprofit creative writing organizations.)

As one example, they purchased a duck tray for $3. With a story, it sold for $71, or 25 times its value. And what did the buyer get for $71?

Duck tray: $3.

Story about the duck tray: $68.

Here's part of that Duck Tray story:

The tray in which he deposited his wallet and keyring and change had been his father's, a period piece which seemed by its design to represent a bygone and overblown masculinity she associated with Anglophile prep schools and stuffy hunt clubs. A painstakingly detailed mallard's head, forged from some cheap metal, rose from the partitioned rosewood dish, as if half of it might be employed as a decoy. Emily had never liked the duck, as they called it, despite its sentimental origins, but now that Henry was gone, she couldn't part with it.

The stories made the difference. The stories themselves have measurable value.

Your Donors' Search for Meaning

In the final scene of *Saving Private Ryan*, our protagonist, after reflecting on the long life he has lived, the legacy he has created with his children and their grandchildren, finally visits the grave of his friend who sacrificed his life to save his.

Kneeling in front of the white cross marking the grave of his fallen comrade, he says: "Every day I think about what you said to me that day on the bridge. And I've tried to live my life the best I could. I hope that was enough. I hope that at least in your eyes, I've earned what all of you have done for me." His wife makes her way among the thousands of graves to his side. He stands, requesting "Tell me I'm a good man."

This desire to live a meaningful life is something we all share. Donors give because they want to feel like they matter. They want that sense of meaning. And giving gives them that sense of meaning.

We all recognize that with many products, in fact most of what we buy, a large part of what we pay is for their intangible benefits—how the products will make us feel.

But what about your nonprofit? When donors give, they have nothing to show for it. Nothing they can point to, touch, or smell, like my son's new sneakers. What are you really selling? And what are your donors really buying?

"John, our donors give because they are generous."

Maybe so, but then why don't they give if no one else is giving? If they're so generous, then why are they reluctant to be the first person to give to your fundraiser?

Are your donors any more altruistic than the average Jane? Maybe so, but what about donors who give to cancer organizations because they feel it lowers their own chances of getting cancer. Crazy, huh?

Donors give because:

- They feel like their gift will have a meaningful impact
- Others like them are also giving
- They feel the project will be successful

Giving your donors opportunities to live with meaning is a sacred act. And this is what you are selling.

A Few CARE Reminders

As we wrap up this section of the book, here are a couple of important reminders before we jump in deeper with each element:

CARE starts from the inside. Ultimately, CARE is an attitude. CARE is human; it begins with how you feel about your work, and how you feel about your donors.

CARE starts from the top. Ultimately, CARE needs to manifest from the executive leadership and board. It's a culture shift that we'll cover later in the book.

CARE only exists in action. Connect, Appreciate, Reply, Encourage. These are all verbs, aren't they? They will only exist to the extent that you do something. CARE doesn't stop. CARE keeps going.

CARE is not lipstick on a pig. Better donor communications will not fix programs that are destined to fail, poor financial management, lousy hiring decisions, etc.

Now, let's take a closer look at each element of CARE.

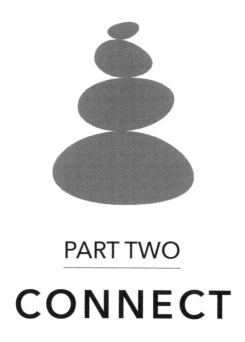

PART TWO

CONNECT

Introduction

We write for the same reason that we walk, talk, climb mountains, or swim the oceans—because we can. We have some impulse within us that makes us want to explain ourselves to other human beings.
—Maya Angelou

Joey is our cat. She's named after Josephine Baker, the African-American dancer who was also a decorated World War II spy and a civil rights activist. Basically, she was the Beyoncé of the 30s and 40s. No doubt, she stood out.

Joey doesn't have quite the legacy of Baker, but she can be a diva. Especially when she wants to be fed or petted, which of course, is always on her terms. She is unique in many ways, but her greeting is like any other ordinary domesticated cat. Whenever she wants to say "Hi" or more accurately, to be seen, she raises her tail straight up in the air and sends up a shiver, causing it to vibrate from the base of her tail all the way up to the tip.

According to Desmond Morris, author of *Catlore*, an erect tail with its whole length quivering "appears to have the meaning of a friendly personal identification, as if the cat is saying, 'Yes, this is me!'"

Yes, this is me. If cats have a sense of identity, and a desire to greet others, then other animals like dogs, elephants, and dolphins must have their own way of saying, "Yes, this is me!"

We humans certainly have ways of signaling individuality and inviting connection in our language, both verbal and non-verbal. But because we are social, "Yes, this is me" is also expressed in the clothes we wear, the friends we keep, and the causes we support. We are all profoundly hard-wired to express our individuality while at the same time claiming membership to particular groups.

When your donors donate money, volunteer, or support in any way, they are expressing, "Yes, this is me." Acknowledging this primal expression makes them feel heard, makes them feel counted, and makes them feel connected.

Let's look at several ways to build and honor those connections.

CHAPTER 6

Why Stories Connect Best with Donors

When someone says to you, "Hey, let's connect," what comes to mind? Heart or mind? Feelings or thoughts?

Connecting is an endeavor of the heart, not the mind. Connections between people are the glue of every social unit—from friends, couples, families, neighborhoods, cities, etc. You might even say connecting is the most human thing you can do. Connecting cuts to the core of what makes us truly human.

But wait. What exactly are these connections made of? We can't touch or see "connection" but we've all had the experience, the feeling, of connection with other people. We also know that connections are something we share with one or more people.

According to Yuval Noah Harari, author of *Sapiens—A Brief History of Humankind*, stories are what make people feel connected with each other, especially large groups. And storytelling is unique to humans—no other animal relies on stories to survive. Harari writes that "large numbers of strangers can cooperate successfully by believing in common myths. Any large-scale human cooperation—whether a modern state, a medieval church, an ancient city or an archaic tribe—is rooted in common myths that exist only in people's collective imagination."

We are the stories we tell.

Whether told face-to-face with a major donor, in a thank-you video, or in your fundraising emails, stories are the most powerful tool in your fundraising and marketing arsenal. That's because, as Harari suggests, human beings are hardwired for storytelling.

Jonathan Gottschall, author of *The Storytelling Animal* agrees: "We are, as a species, addicted to story. Even when the body goes to sleep, the mind stays up all night, telling itself stories."

Stories act like a lock-and-key mechanism to get attention, ignite motivation, and invite action.

The Woman Who Fell Down The Well

One of charity: water's most successful fundraising campaigns was about a mother from Niger named Aissa Marou. Collecting water is a responsibility that falls solely on the women. Mothers are not exempt. They must carry babies on their backs as they make the journey back and forth from the well, using handmade ropes and wooden buckets to perform this backbreaking task for hours each day.

One day, while Aissa was collecting water from the local well, she lost her balance. Aissa and her baby fell into the well.

To prove just how powerful storytelling is, I won't tell you how Aissa's story ends. I bet you feel frustrated or even angry that I left you hanging. Your brain is aching for a resolution to the story. You might drop this book and use Google to find out how it ends. You may even make a donation to charity: water to help mothers like Aissa.

This story from charity: water is just one example of how compelling storytelling can be for fundraising. In fact, storytelling is the very foundation of every successful marketing and fundraising campaign.

The Right Stories Make Fundraising Hormones Surge

There is a mountain of research, some of which you've probably read, that has already proven the powerful role storytelling can play in your fundraising and donor communications. Storytelling is the most powerful tool in your fundraising arsenal. It's not statistics, it's not theory, it's not slick technology. It's a story. You can have the best strategies, tactics, and tech, but without a good fundraising story, every campaign will fall flat on its face.

Let's do an experiment that demonstrates how storytelling changes your brain chemistry. It will be fun!

I want you to read the following two stories out loud to yourself, inspired by the work of Dr. Paul Zak, whom I will tell you more about in just a moment. Notice how you FEEL when you read each story.

Story #1: To celebrate Ben's 5th birthday, he and his father take a trip to the zoo. His father whisks him up on his shoulders as they pass the black and white striped zebra, the tall giraffe, the silly chimpanzees, and the big fat hippos. They see many other wonderful animals during their visit, many of which Ben had never seen before—even on TV. After filling up on cotton candy, Ben declares, "This is the best birthday ever!" Later, as Ben is drifting off to sleep, he dreams about many of the animals he saw at the zoo.

How did you feel? Probably warm and fuzzy. You may remember your own visit to a zoo with your dad when you were young.

Story #2: To celebrate Ben's 5th birthday, his father announces a surprise in the backyard. A brand new swing set! Ben squeals with delight as he struggles to lift himself up onto the swing, which is just a bit too high for his little legs. After his father gives Ben a lift, he gently pushes him from behind. Ben squeals, "Higher, higher!" His father yearns to share the joy that Ben feels, but he only feels sad. That's because he knows something that Ben doesn't know. And that is that Ben will likely be dead in one year from brain cancer. Each moment he spends with Ben is infinitely more precious than the previous moment. It's as if he himself is dying along with his son.

How did you feel when you read this story? Probably not the same as when you read the first story. Most likely, you felt sad and anxious. You may have even felt a need to help Ben.

What was the difference between these two stories? And why did you feel differently with each story?

Dr. Paul Zak, who studies the neurochemical roots of human decision-making had these same questions. So he conducted an experiment to determine how each story affected the brain chemistry.

He discovered that two hormones flooded the brains of participants after hearing a story about a boy who was dying of brain cancer. The first hormone was oxytocin, which is associated with feelings of empathy, care and connection. The second was cortisol, which is associated with distress.

Additionally, these subjects had higher heart rates and respiratory rates, further demonstrating distress in response to the story about the boy when he was dying of brain cancer.

He also discovered that participants who produced oxytocin and cortisol were more likely to donate money to a charity that helps sick children. Further, he was able to predict how much money people would give based on the level of oxytocin and cortisol detected in blood tests.

Stories connect, and stories raise money.

CHAPTER 7

Stories Connect Donors with Problems to Solve

As this experiment in the last chapter illustrates, you can't maximize your fundraising narrative without a problem for your donors to solve (like childhood cancer). Your story must make people feel the pain of being cast out, marginalized, or physically threatened.

Connecting Donors with Their Impact

Notice that I wrote "their" impact. Donors want to solve problems and create impact. Most organizations I've worked with have a problem with connecting their donors directly to the impact. Some feel that it's unfair to their program people. Others think that it's misleading when the donor is actually giving the organization the money to create the impact. Still, others don't understand why donors can't just be happy with giving money to their awesome nonprofit and leaving it at that.

All of the fundraising research into the psychology behind why donors give points to one thing: It's all about them.

But it's also about the things you share. Connection is sharing, like sharing chocolate, or a movie. Connection allows you and that other person to share something you both have in common. Connection means you belong.

The Truth of Why We Give

Think about the last time you made a donation to your favorite charity. It made you feel good because you were taking action on something you believed in. You may even have felt the rush of oxytocin just after making a gift. You gave because it's meaningful to you.

Donors don't give because they are generous and are thinking about someone else. Yes, everyone likes to think that about themselves—but ultimately people act and give money to an organization because they want to feel a certain way. Again, it's about the feeling and the experience, not the money, and certainly not about your organization and how effective it is.

Connecting the donor to the impact means that your narrative makes the donor the hero. Your nonprofit is *not* the hero. Donors will give less if you insert yourself in between them and the impact that they seek. The structure of your narrative should put the donor in the role of the hero. And what does the hero do? The hero saves the day!

Batman Doesn't Donate

Batman saves the city, the victim in distress, or the bus that's teetering on the bridge. You want to do the same thing for your donors. You want to make them Batman. You don't do this by telling donors to "donate." Of course, they are giving you money so it's natural that the word "donate" would seem appropriate. But there's much more to it than that.

Donors don't give because they're generous. They give because it feels great. And being a hero feels the best. This isn't just unicorn thinking. It's a phenomenon that's hard-wired deeply in the human brain from millions of years of evolution. (Yay, science!) When you tell donors they can "feed hungry children," "stop human trafficking," or "give twice the hope," you make them the hero.

Donors give because they want to change the world. They want to be the hero. Isn't that true with you?

Impact Should Match the Heart and the Wallet

During my cancer treatment, I came to be known as the "Lion King." Actually, I was a self-described Lion King. I told people that I am undefeated like the Lion King. The Lion King is only king precisely because he is undefeated by every single enemy in the forest. The Lion King never gives up. No matter what may happen, no matter how many scars, the Lion King remains the king of the jungle.

When I saw the opportunity from the San Francisco Zoo to adopt an animal, guess which one I chose? The lion, of course! Honestly, I probably wouldn't donate any money to the San Francisco Zoo normally as there are many zoos closer to me that I could easily support. However, I was the Lion! Adopting a lion connected to me more personally. The lion is part of my story.

Adopting the lion was also a fundraising "product" with stories around it, including your donor's own stories, just like my Lion King story. Specificity and timing matter.

73

The offer also has to match the budget of the donor. I'm not a millionaire so I'm not going to make a big deal, but I'm very likely to adopt one of their animals.

The more general and vague your offer is, the less likely donors will be interested. The more specific your requests, the more likely donors will feel connected to it. Batman needs to know who or what to save.

Getting out of the Way of the Story

At the same time you make the donor the hero, you also have to remove your organization from any unnecessary mention within that narrative. For example, instead of saying, "Thank you so much for giving money to our organization so that we can change the world," you want to say, "Thank you so much for making a difference in a child's life." See how the organization is removed from that narrative?

If you're asking, "John, how will the donor know that our organization is the one who is involved?" don't worry, it's obvious. Donors know the organization they are giving money to. It's in your email header. Your organization's name is all over your appeal, the return envelope, the reply letter, the newsletter, social media, your website. Your organization's brand is all over the place. But inserting your brand between the donor and the impact they seek will inhibit giving. It takes the wind out of the donor's sail.

Here are a few examples of removing your organization from your fundraising narrative, thus making your donor communications more impactful:

1. Avoid bragging about your nonprofit in your donor communications. Instead, brag about the donor.

2. Use second person narrative. "You" instead of "we" or "us." Exception: First person narratives with donor or beneficiary voices can be great stories.

3. Tell the donor what they did in terms of impact, not what your nonprofit will do with their money.

4. Report back to the donor about the impact they made with their gift.

5. Reinforce the idea that your donors matter. Reinforce this truth as consistently and as frequently as possible.

Personalization and Impact

Donors will give more if you treat them as individuals and if you acknowledge the unique relationship that they have with your organization. But how can you scale this?

This is where the magic of personalization comes into play.

What is personalization? Personalization means that you were sending the right message to the right person, based on their relationship with you. For example, if they recently donated to your organization, they are a new donor. What does a new donor want to hear about? They want to hear an acknowledgment. They want to feel appreciated. They want to know that their gift was received and it will be put to good use immediately. They want to hear about their impact.

Of course, you can write a personal email to them, but that does not scale. Instead, you should use your email marketing to set up automation that uses their first name, ties them to the project they are funding, and tells them what the next step is as a new donor (e.g., like our Facebook page, join our Facebook group, share the fundraising campaign with your friends, etc.)

Personalization also means letting donors choose what they want to get from you. For example, let them choose various different types of content to receive by email or direct mail. Of course, you have to have the technology to keep track of these preferences.

CHAPTER 8

Elements of Great Fundraising Stories

Yes, good stories raise money. But where do you start with YOUR storytelling? Maybe you're thinking, "John, I'm not that creative type. I'm not a natural storyteller." Well, I would argue that because you're human you are a "natural storyteller." Still, I see your point and it's a common feeling shared by many accidental marketers and nonprofit communicators. They just don't know how to structure a good fundraising story. I'll show you how right now.

There are four elements of every successful story. I call them the four Ps.

1. The Person

If a story doesn't hook the reader or listener in the first few seconds, it won't move people to take action. To put people in motion, you have to trigger an emotion. You do this by first making people feel empathy or connection to a person. The grandmother who's fighting breast cancer so that she can be at her grandchild's high school graduation. The spirited 5-year old boy dying of brain cancer. The mother who breaks her back every day just to collect drinking water for her child. Connect your donor to a person.

2. The Problem

Great stories hold our attention after we're emotionally hooked. We continue to pay attention as long as there are problems and unanswered questions about the progression of the story. The story about Ben only got our attention and focus when we learned he was going to die from brain cancer.

Jonathan Gottschall, author of *The Storytelling Animal* argues that all stories by definition have problems. He writes that the "problem structure reveals a major function of storytelling. It suggests that the human mind was shaped for story, so that it could be shaped by story."

Five-year-old Ben and his father triggered feelings of love and empathy. His early death from brain cancer made you feel anxious and uncomfortable, wanting to do anything to help.

3. The Payoff

The payoff is the resolution to the plot questions, and thus, the story. Like problems, the payoff is so essential to every story, that without it, you really don't have a story at all. "Once upon a time" without "happily ever after" is like "left" without "right."

In terms of your fundraising narrative, the payoff is the call-to-action. The payoff is the punchline to the person and problem.

Remember, the goal is to make the donor the hero, not your organization.

How do you feel when you read the following statements aloud?

- Give clean water
- Feed hungry children
- Stop human trafficking
- Stand with immigrants

Each of these asks is associated with a problem (dirty water, hungry children, etc.) which triggers empathy. The donor, who wants to be the hero, ultimately seeks to make a meaningful impact more than they seek to part with their money.

4. The Pump Up

No, it's not an item on Jet Blue's menu. Instead, the pump up is all about generating a good feeling and positive experience for the donor after they make a gift. The pump up is all about telling the donor what they did and why they are so amazing. Appreciation is the essence of the pump up.

But Where Do My Statistics Go?

Most nonprofits love statistics. They remind staff and board members why their work matters. And statistics can be helpful when reporting outcomes or applying for grants.

But using statistics can often hurt your fundraising appeals. Statistics can turn an emotionally compelling appeal into a total bummer.

In the Power of One study by Paul Slovic at the University of Oregon, two groups of potential donors were each asked to give money to help end hunger. The first group was asked to give money to help a little girl suffering from hunger. The second group was asked to help the same little girl, but were also told about the millions of other children also suffering from hunger.

The results were surprising: Even though the second group was presented with a greater need (millions of hungry children), they gave half as much money as the first group.

But why? Why do people who are naturally endowed with rational thinking give less when presented with statistics demonstrating a huge need?

According to researcher Paul Slovic, the good feeling from helping the starving girl gets contaminated with the bad feeling about millions of starving people: "If our brain … creates an illusion of non-efficacy, people could be demotivated by thinking, 'Well, this is such a big problem. Is my donation going to be effective in any way?'"

Statistics actually compete with the good feelings that your fundraising appeal produces. Donors give because of how awesome it makes them feel. Statistics make donors feel less good, causing them to give less.

This isn't to say that statistics aren't helpful with fundraising. They're just more useful as a footnote, or as part of an FAQ, not as the headline.

Happy Stories and Sad Stories: Which Connects Better?

Will you raise more money with happy stories of success? Or will sad stories raise more?

One powerful study tested whether happy or sad faces worked best in charity ads. Researchers discovered that highly involved supporters (donors, volunteers, supporters, etc.) preferred to see happy faces, whereas people who were relatively uninvolved preferred sad faces.

So it depends.

More people give when they are emotionally driven to solve a problem (sad). And they stay involved when they see their impact making a difference (happy).

I asked my friend Julie Edwards at the Humane Society of Northeast Georgia what she thought about happy versus sad fundraising stories and here's what she said:

"Our number one fundraising story to date was, of course, the Habersham rescue, a horrific 350+ dog puppy mill case which was incredibly sad and raised about $12K."

The Sad-Happy Story Cycle

In fundraising communications, sad stories and happy stories generally follow the donor communications cycle: ASK, THANK, REPORT BACK.

1. ASK: When you want to ask donors to give, you tell a sad story.
2. THANK: When they donate, you immediately thank them and tell them a happy story of what their give is doing.
3. REPORT BACK: When you update donors about their awesome impact (happy story), you also have to remind them that more work needs to be done (sad story).

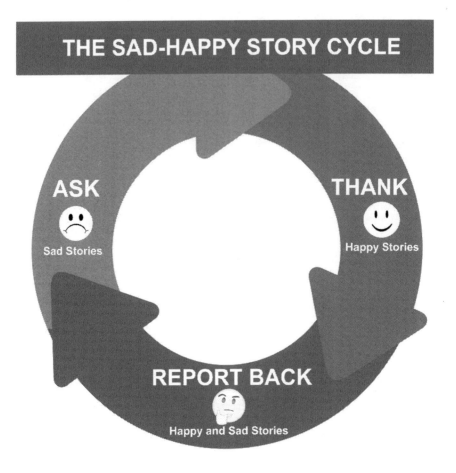

See, you can tell a great fundraising story after all!

CHAPTER 9

Content That Builds Connections with Donors

Stories are wonderful, but there are other ways that your communications can connect with donors too.

Connecting Donors with Useful Resources

Mercy for Animals has an entire website devoted to promoting veganism called Choose Veg. My favorite part of this website are the recipes, of course. This site also has a vegan meal planner, tips on switching to veganism, and more.

Admittedly, I'm not much of a foodie, and prefer recipes with three ingredients or less and three steps or less. I don't live to eat, I eat to live. So this website provides a lot of immediate and specific value and utility. It literally helps me save time and live a healthy life. Of course the website doesn't give me everything I need to save time and live a healthier life, but it does give me something very specific—something I find very useful.

I donate to Mercy for Animals. But not for the recipes. They share a lot of my values in terms of the dignity of all life, cows, chickens, fish, etc.

Occasionally I will eat beef or fish, but I do my best to buy the most humane meats possible, in part from the information I've received from Mercy for Animals and their yummy recipes.

My donation is a reflection of values and my continued support is a reflection of my loyalty to Mercy for Animals.

What kind of value are you creating for your donors?

In *Youtility: Why Smart Marketing Is about Help Not Hype*, Jay Baer writes:

"What if instead of trying to be amazing you just focused on being useful? What if you decided to inform, rather than promote? You know that expression, "If you give a man to fish, you feed him for a day; if you teach a man to fish, you feed him for a lifetime?" Well the same is true for marketing: if you sell something, you make a customer today; if you help someone, you make a customer for life."

Almost every single nonprofit I've worked with has a storehouse of expertise and valuable information that will help their donors become better fisherwomen. These resources will create real, immediate value in the lives of your donors, and they are often right under your nose in your laptop! Here are some examples:

Animal shelters have pet care tips

Education foundations have teaching tips for parents

Cancer foundations help caregivers balance their personal health with the needs of a loved one

For more on creating value with content, please devour Kivi Leroux Miller's book, *Content Marketing for Nonprofits*.

Connecting Donors with Their Community

Fight Colorectal Cancer (Fight CRC) ambassadors spend huge chunks of their lives telling their stories and speaking out about colorectal cancer. They attend training conferences, speak at events, and invest their time in countless other activities—all to prevent untimely deaths from colorectal cancer.

Most Fight CRC ambassadors are colorectal cancer survivors, challenged every day with pain, fatigue, and side effects from treatment. Which begs the question: Why do they spend their limited time and energy as ambassadors?

This is the exact question I had when I was hired to help Fight CRC promote their ambassador program. When I interviewed veteran ambassadors, I asked this question and wasn't surprised by their answers.

Cancer can be a very lonely experience. I can say this personally. Although family, friends, colleagues do their best to support, ultimately I am the one facing cancer. I am the one facing my mortality more directly and intimately than anyone around me. There are so many things I experience, and my friends, family, colleagues couldn't possibly understand. And that's natural; they don't have cancer.

You have to have it to really get it. The fatigue, the despair, the brain fog, the metal taste on your teeth, the constant ringing in the ears, the insomnia. Whenever I go to Dana-Farber, I have comrades. They get it. They know exactly what I'm going through, how it feels. And we are fighting together. There's a unity in our shared struggle. There's a home. There's a connection.

During my interviews, I found that, like me, these cancer survivors expressed their gratitude and fortune for finding their people, their community.

Several Fight CRC ambassadors reported to me during the project that the greatest benefit they received by becoming an advocate was finally finding their family. They found people with a shared struggle, a deep connection.

This is the kind of connection you create when you connect supporters with each other. Whether they are dog lovers, cancer survivors, parents of autistic children, sexual abuse survivors, etc., the value you create is this connection.

Stop trying to be the source of great information and start being a useful resource. Start helping donors find their communities.

I once worked with a very small organization intent on being the sole expert for everything Amyotrophic Lateral Sclerosis (ALS) for caregivers, for patients, for family members. With a small staff, I knew that they could not keep up. So we changed their social media strategy. I help them shift from trying to be the source of all information to trying to be a resource that encourages caregivers.

For instance, instead of sharing a tip to reduce muscle tension and leaving it at that, they took it one step further. They still shared a tip but also asked, "This is one way to reduce muscle tension. What's your top tip for reducing muscle tension?" See the shift? It goes from being a source to being a resource that leverages the community together to find the best solution. After all, family members, patients, and caregivers are really the experts!

Connecting donors with their community creates value in three ways:

1. Banishes isolation
2. Shares stories
3. Shares resources

Connecting donors with the community, in the end, makes your organization look great and obviously enhances your brand.

Connect with First-Time Donors with a Welcome Series

Ready for a really easy way to boost donor retention that not nearly enough nonprofits are taking advantage of? Connect early by setting up a three-part donor welcome series in six easy steps.

1. Set a Clear Goal for the Series

Decide what you want new donors to do next. Do you want new donors to share the campaign they just donated to with their friends? Do you want them to like your Facebook Page? Do you want them to learn more about the cause?

2. Segment Your Donors

In your welcome series, your audience is pretty clear: people who just made a donation for the first time. But you may need to customize your messages for different kinds of donors so they speak to the specific relationship. For example, a welcome email to a new monthly donor should reinforce the long-term impact of their support.

3. Make It About Them

Each email in the series should create value for the donor.

Thanking the donor, reminding them of their impact, and asking for feedback all create value in the heart of the donor. In short, it's about making them feel like they matter—that they are important.

4. Determine Message Frequency

You have to strike a balance between reminding donors about upcoming campaigns and being too pushy. The first email should go out immediately, but when to send the remaining emails in your series may vary. The secret is to focus on another opportunity to make an impact rather than asking for more money.

5. Write Your Email Series

Keep your emails brief and in the second-person, as if you're writing to a friend. Consider this series:

- Message 1—Welcome new donors, reinforce their decision to give.
- Message 2—Update the donors on their impact, ask for their feedback (a quick survey).
- Message 3—Invite donors to give again, or upgrade to a monthly donor.

6. Set It and (Almost) Forget It

The best thing about an email welcome series is that you can "set it and forget it." The series is automatically initiated by the donor. But you still need to monitor opens and clicks for each message to make sure they're working.

For example, if your open rate is 60 percent, that's good. But if your click rate is only 5 percent, you need to work on the body of that message (copy, image, action calls).

CHAPTER 11

Connect Now with Live Video

One of the best ways to connect your community together and create the most value is also the scariest: Live video.

Live video (available on all the popular social networks) allows you to do something that you've never done before: Provide live unprecedented access to stories, happenings, the community, and resources.

It allows you to be here now with your community. It's also an excellent way to create tremendous engagement on any of these social platforms, simply because it is real-time, and as they engage, the algorithms send those engagement signals out to their friends in real-time. The more you engage people during your broadcast, the more they show up during the broadcast.

Although live broadcasting is simple to use, you may feel understandably hesitant about unscripted content marketing.

Common fears and concerns I've heard over the years:
- What are we going to talk about?
- How should we respond to commenters?
- How long should we broadcast?
- Will anybody actually tune-in?

If you have clear objectives and a plan that makes sense, you'll be more successful using Facebook Live or other live video to engage with supporters.

Here are a few tips to get you started.

Don't Freak Out

Mistakes will be made. No matter how much you prepare, every now and then something goes wrong. This is especially true when trying something for the first time like Facebook Live.

You will feel nervous—everyone feels nervous the first time they're on live video. Take a deep breath and just do it. Even if everything goes totally wrong, you will still live. You will survive this.

Pick a Topic People Want to Discuss

Obviously, you want to pick a topic that people want to discuss. The more specific and relevant your topic is to the viewer, the better. Here are some suggestions:

- Trending topics or news
- Frequently asked questions about a specific problem or topic
- Show people what goes on behind the scenes—how donors make impact
- Important themes your community is already talking about on social media

Tell People When You're Going Live

Live video isn't that exciting if no one shows up. To make sure your core supporters show up when you go live:

- Post an update on your page the week before and the day before
- Send an email that morning with a link to your broadcast
- Share future broadcasts dates and topics in your email newsletter
- Share your broadcast across all social channels immediately before you go live

Make an Outline for Your Broadcast

A written outline will be your security blanket. Even though live video seems off the cuff, the best live videos have an outline behind them.

Here's a sample:

- In the first five seconds answer, "What's in it for me?" (the viewer).
- Introduce yourself
- Thank your viewers sincerely for making time
- Outline the questions or topics you will cover
- Deliver the content
- Tell people what's next

Write a Compelling Description

When you're ready to go live, you will be prompted to write a description for your broadcast. Keep it short, clear, and compelling. Sell it!

Respond to Commenters

The best thing about live broadcasting is seeing comments posted in real-time. This is a unique opportunity to engage supporters in a dialogue that creates value for everyone!

- Be cheerful
- Call out commenters by name
- Reply to their comment
- Say thank you

Share the Broadcast Again and Again

You've put a lot of time and effort into your first live broadcast. Congratulations! Make sure this investment goes further by sharing it with your supporters.

- Send a follow-up email
- Link to the broadcast in your newsletter
- Reshare the broadcast on your Page
- Tell them when your next broadcast will be

Repurpose the Recording

Always save the recording file when prompted at the end of your broadcast. Again, there are so many ways to make this content live on and on:

- Slice it up into smaller videos (60 seconds or less for Instagram).
- Transcribe the audio for blog posts (Transcription services are very affordable these days.)
- Edit and use the audio for a podcast—especially if you've developed a weekly theme for your broadcast like what I

did with the Hump Day Coffee Break, which has over 100 broadcasts: facebook.com/pg/JohnHaydon.Marketing/videos

I love doing live videos because they make it so easy to connect with people. I bet you will, too . . . once you give them a try.

PART THREE

APPRECIATE

Introduction

'Thank You' is a miraculous expression. We feel good when we say it, and we feel good when we hear it.
—Daisaku Ikeda

At the beginning of my cancer treatment, I started with an immunotherapy drug in clinical trials which seemed to work beautifully. It hacked my immune system to attack the cancer cells. However, three months after I started treatment, I began experiencing shortness of breath.

I chalked this up to a side effect from the treatment, but my symptoms continued to get worse until early one morning, I was startled awake from a nightmare.

In the nightmare, three hideous devil-like creatures were dragging me by the feet down a long dark hallway. I tried desperately to grip onto anything—walls, door handles—but everything I grabbed just slipped through my hands. Everything was moving by so fast.

I was scared, but I was also filled with rage.

"No!" I screamed. They were not going to take me down this hallway. Suddenly, I found myself awake and felt a strange sensation in my chest. I felt my pulse skipping every three or four beats. My heartbeat was very irregular and very weak. Kate called my oncologist, and he urged us to go to the emergency room right away.

I was hooked up to all types of machines to monitor my heart through the night. That plus my anxiety meant that I was not able to sleep at all. I'm a Buddhist, so I used my Buddhist chanting to bring courage out of my life. I went on a profound spiritual journey during the night, thinking about what really mattered in my life. At one point, I felt at peace, like I wouldn't die. I felt confident that, even if I had a heart attack, I was in the best possible place to have a heart attack.

I also felt a tremendous sense of appreciation for my life itself. Even though this could be the end of my life, I felt gratitude for every moment. I felt thankful for having cancer in the first place because it enabled me to dramatically transform how I looked at my life.

The next day, I was surprisingly delighted to get started with the procedure to drain fluid away from my heart, with no worries at all. It was as if my life expanded to become larger than the obstacle, which was so scary the night before. I even felt confident, encouraging the doctors, telling jokes, and asking them about their families. I was not only fearless, I was invincible.

And I healed, very quickly. This makes complete scientific sense because our bodies are literally 99.99999 percent energy. This is why many cancer researchers agree that anger and fear impair the immune system, why positive feelings like gratitude and hopeful expectations enhance our immune system.

According to holistic medicine guru Joe Dispenza, gratitude actually tricks one's biology into thinking that it has already received the benefit of healing. "Gratitude causes the body to experience a biological upgrade. In the process, an enormous amount of physiological changes take place causing the body to reorganize itself on a cellular level," says Joe.

CHAPTER 12

Appreciation is a Feeling, Not a Job

To get through the most challenging time, the trick for me is not just thinking about being grateful, but **feeling** grateful. I must put my entire body in a state of deep gratitude, as if I've already received the benefit I should be thankful for. Whenever I'm in this state, I heal faster. To me, and to science, gratitude is that powerful. Gratitude became my superpower on that day and continued to be my #1 superpower throughout my cancer treatment.

We've all heard the phrase "an attitude of gratitude." But until I got cancer, I thought it was just a clever memorable little phrase to remind us to be thankful. Of course it's easy to be thankful when things are going well. But to me, the real power of gratitude is demonstrated when things aren't going well. In my case, spiritual transformation was required. Gratitude transformed my inner state from victimhood and fear into a protagonist with power.

Think about the times you've felt grateful. It's a feeling, right? It fills your entire body with such positive energy. Gratitude is not about thinking—it's deeper. It's about your spiritual intent.

A 2003 study called *Counting Blessings Versus Burdens: An Experimental Investigation of Gratitude and Subjective Well-Being in Daily Life* by the University of Miami and the University of California demonstrated the biological and psychological power of gratitude. The study showed that an attitude of gratitude increased well-being, concluding that "a conscious focus on blessings may have emotional and interpersonal benefits." Participants weren't more grateful than the average person, and didn't have more reasons to be more grateful than the average person. They simply took action to practice gratitude in their daily life by shifting their focus.

Gratitude Can Transform Your Nonprofit

Gratitude isn't something that's limited to our personal lives. The spiritual aspect of gratitude within our life penetrates the lives of other people, including our coworkers and our donors.

After my awakening to the power of gratitude, it hit me: Feeling grateful is key to thanking donors. For donors to feel it, it must be sincere—it must be truly felt by the person who is doing the thanking.

It starts with a mindset. If your only goal for thanking donors is to get another donation, then you're missing the point. Gratitude transforms relationships, and is the essence of reciprocity, likability, and increased value. That last part, value, goes way beyond funds raised.

I'm a big fan and supporter of the Humane Society of Northeast Georgia (HSNEGA). The staff has an unbelievable commitment to rescuing and saving animals, regardless of the time of day or night, even on days off. Julie Edwards, the executive director, even skipped spending Father's Day with her dad when the HSNEGA received an urgent call to rescue several small adult dogs from a backyard breeder. In the end, her amazing 78-year old dad was one of the only volunteers who stepped up for the last-minute 10+ hour round trip to rescue the dogs because he didn't want the dogs to wait another day for someone to help them.

Of course, this gargantuan love for animals is not unique to HSNEGA. The same level of commitment is demonstrated by humane societies all across the United States, including the Animal Rescue League of Boston where I live. But I consistently support HSNEGA as a monthly donor, give whenever I can when asked during special appeals, and when you can only pick one organization for a Facebook fundraiser for your birthday, I chose HSNEGA.

Why am I such a rabid (pardon the pun) fan of HSNEGA? Because of the way they say "thank you." I've received a few handwritten thank-you cards, a donor newsletter telling me how amazing I am because of the impact I made in the life of a doggo, and have been praised and thanked all over social media for my support.

The Effort of Thanking Conveys Sincerity

Over the past few years, Julie Edwards with HSNEGA has also become a personal friend of mine, which has been incredibly valuable during my cancer journey. One day, when I called to say Hi and catch up, I realized after a few minutes that I caught her at a busy moment, even though it was after working hours. Finally, I asked, "Did I catch you at a bad time?"

She was, of course, busy writing thank-you notes to a few new donors. Among the many tasks that hit her desk every day, thanking donors is a priority for Julie. When asked why thanking donors is very much on her front burner, she replied: "It works. It costs almost nothing but time. And a heartfelt thank you is the best gift you can give a supporter."

Many organizations have forgotten to treat each donor as if they were the most important donor in the world. So thanking donors is sometimes seen as obligatory. Like a box to be ticked in a checklist.

When a donor makes that first gift, how you thank them can either develop that relationship or not. They may have given in response to a natural disaster, and may never return. Or maybe they gave because they're seeking to do something—anything—after their mom just passed from breast cancer. Whatever the case may be, how you thank them will set the tone for the near future.

Going Beyond the Thankless Thank You

When donors give, it's never about the money. It's never because they have extra money to blow after they've paid the bills, and given back to themselves with dinner and a movie, a short vacation, or a impulse Instagram purchase. Giving is always about the meaningful impact donors seek to create in a world with so much bad news.

Giving is almost always personal. Giving is ultimately a way for the donor to write their own story. We'd like to believe that giving is a selfless act; it is to some degree. But giving is selfish, too. My mom survived a brain aneurysm when I was a child. When I support brain aneurysm nonprofits, it's always because making that sort of impact helps me change my story. I go from being a passive victim devastated by my mom's aneurysm to the narrator, director, writer, hero, etc. I rewrite my history through giving.

Thanking donors for their gift because you think they're generous is not correct. That level of thanking is no different than a Peet's barista who thanks you for buying a plain donut and a black coffee. It's a habit. It's obligatory.

The real power of appreciating donors is recognizing that they have a story. They always have a story. And even if we don't know the details of that story, appreciating that they are giving because it's personal (it always is) allows you to feel appreciation. Do you really feel it though? In your heart, do you hold them close? When you can bring yourself into that state, from thinking to feeling appreciation, magical things will happen.

Appreciation is an active process that increases the value of that donor in your heart. Just like a house that appreciates, increases in value, your relationship with your donor—the feeling you have and the feeling they experience—is enhanced.

It's like the grinch whose heart grew ten times bigger when he saw for the first time how generous and kind the citizens of Whoville were.

When we feel appreciative, we change—we feel bigger—and our donors also feel that. They feel your heart growing ten times bigger. Why? Because your ten-times heart now approaches how you thank donors. Your thank-you emails, your thank-you notes, every way you thank the donor becomes 10 times bigger because your intent changed. This is the essence of the oneness of fundraiser and donors. Both people are changed, and it starts with you!

I know you get it. You've no doubt already had experiences of how you thank donors when you've felt your heart grow 10 times bigger because you've stepped into a new heart-space of appreciation for your donors.

You've also had experiences where you are lacking in appreciation, like when you're too busy or burned out. It happens to all of us; we're only human. When our hearts contract and shrink, our state of life is contracted and small. In that state, we can't appreciate our donors. And our actions never fail to reflect that state.

We rubber-stamp thank-you notes, without care and attention. We make mistakes. We may even put off or forget to send a thank-you email. And our thank-you message lacks the appreciation that's required to grow the relationship we really want with our donors.

Again, the oneness of fundraiser and donor are at work. A contracted heart of appreciation causes the entire thank-you experience to implode—it can even lead to begrudging our donors!

How you feel about your donors penetrates your staff, processes, and policies. How you feel will always be revealed. This is the oneness of self and other, fundraiser and donor.

Levels and Stages of Thanking

How to say thanks depends on your relationship with the person being thanked. You wouldn't thank a Lyft driver for getting you to your destination on time in the same way you'd thank your dad on Father's Day. Unless your Lyft driver is also your dad.

Thanking should also reflect the different types of relationships you have with your donors. You'd thank a diehard major donor very differently than a donor who makes a $25 gift for the very first time. But remember, it's not about the money. Thanking is different not because one gave $25,000 and the other gave $25. Thanking is different because of the relationship the donor has with your organization. Specifically the level of commitment they've expressed in their giving.

Sometimes thanking is about the immediate impact the donor made, sometimes it's about the greater cause, and sometimes it's even about you.

In 2018, the Institute for Conversational Fundraising, Pursuant, and Bloomerang sponsored a research project titled "Learning to Say Thank-You: The Role of Donor Acknowledgments." This study took a deep dive into thank you acknowledgment purposes and practices.

Level 1: An acknowledgment serving as a receipt of a gift.

Level 2: An acknowledgment to create a good feeling associated with any action a person takes for an organization.

Level 3: An acknowledgment communication may generate measurable behavioral benefits in increasing giving.

Level 4: An acknowledgment communication may generate measurable benefits in increasing the quality of a donor's relationship with an organization.

Level 5: An acknowledgment communication may appreciate the donors as people (not simply what they do for an organization).

The most powerful thing about this study is that it focuses on the positive feelings from being thanked rather than the amount of money given or the number of times a donor gives. Jen Shang, Adrian Sargeant, Kathryn Carpenter, and Harriet Day, the authors of this study write, "If the donor does not feel adequately thanked, the acknowledgment has failed even though it may produce a second gift."

This gets back to the primary purpose of thanking and that is donor stewardship—to develop and grow a relationship.

Many fundraisers consider thanking donors obligatory, something that must follow giving. However, the real power of thanking donors is realized when the goal of thanking is forward-looking, focused on developing and deepening donor loyalty. Thanking is not about the past—it's about the future.

Thanking shouldn't be seen as the effect of the donor's gift, but rather a cause to enhance the future relationship with the donor. Thanking is a cause, not an effect, of the relationship you have with the donor.

CHAPTER 13

Heavy Metal Methods For Thanking Your Donors

In 1979, Black Sabbath, the most famous heavy metal band from England, began a death spiral towards its destruction, culminating with the firing of Ozzy Osbourne.

Doing what any other drugged-out, heavy-drinking, rock-and-roll icon would do, he locked himself in a hotel room for four months. Fortunately, his manager, now wife, shook him awake. She said, "Get your sh*t together and I'll manage you," to which Ozzy replied, "Okay."

This started with looking for a guitar player whom Ozzy could partner with to completely revolutionize his career. But the search was not easy. They went from New York to Los Angeles, all over the United States, and auditioned over 170 guitar players.

Ozzy felt like he'd exhausted everything. But then his friend, Slaughter bassist Dana Strum, who had been helping him the whole time, said, "If you haven't seen Randy Rhoads, then you haven't seen what this town has to offer." The town was Los Angeles.

Randy, on the other hand, was reluctant to audition for Ozzy Osbourne. He was classically trained and was very much interested in classical music and had no interest in playing with a man who seemed like a complete fool to the world.

Finally, at his mother's insistence, Randy decided to audition. He drove up to Malibu and ended up at the hotel where Ozzy was, at 2:00 a.m. in the morning.

Randy showed up with a tiny practice amp and a Flying V guitar, and nothing else.

Randy was surprised. "I thought I was going to play with a band. All I brought was this little Fender tune-up. And they said, 'Okay. Play.' And I thought, 'You've got to be joking. I mean, what could I play?' I didn't have any other musicians with me, so I just started warming up."

Ozzy said, "Yeah. You're good." Randy got the gig. He said later: "Ozzy told me that all the guys who'd auditioned had brought Marshall stacks and Echoplexes. I brought a tiny practice amp. I started tuning up, and he said, 'You got the gig.'"

Although he heard very little of what Randy was capable of, Ozzy knew that what he *was* hearing was the real thing, a guitar player with his own voice. All the other guitar players thought they were a Hendrix clone. They had big hair and big amps. Big peacock feathers.

Here's my point: Are you thanking your donors in a flashy way, showing up with too much, like big hair and Marshall stacks?

If so, you're basically showing up like every other nonprofit, focusing on flash instead of substance. If you are doing that, you're essentially invisible.

If your thank-you notes, your thank-you cards, your thank-you phone calls are unrecognizable and indistinguishable from many other of the same communications your donors receive, you will not stand out.

It's time for you to employ the Randy Rhoads method.

Show up, keep it simple, sincere, from the heart. and create contrast with other organizations. Show up. Keep it simple. Be the real deal and create contrast from the other organizations that are bombarding donors with the same-old, same-old communications.

Simple Ways to Stand Apart in Your Thanking

Give some of these approaches a try.

Spy and learn: Make a small donation to five nonprofits that are your best competition. Pick nonprofits that do similar work in the eyes of your donors (solve homelessness, find homes for dogs, fight cancer, etc). Review how each nonprofit handles your donation experience. Is your nonprofit's thank you as vanilla as theirs was to you?

Do it faster: With marketing automation and the right process, it's totally possible for donors to receive a thank-you email instantly, and a signed thank-you postcard within 48 hours.

Thoughtfulness: Take an extra five minutes with each donor to look what they're saying on social. If so, and if it's relevant, mention that in your postcard. "We noticed that you're planning to hike the white mountains next weekend. Enjoy!"

Connect: Steal what the Humane Society of Northeast Georgia does and connect with your donor's story. Their simple thank-you cards thank me, the donor, for my specific impact on a specific animal. It's my story, my connection!

CHAPTER 14

Create a Thank-You Page Donors Won't Soon Forget

W hile it's true that your website's donation page is mostly responsible for converting donors, your thank-you page plays an equally important role: Retaining those donors.

To increase donor retention, your thank-you page should employ at least five key tactics.

1. Track Donor Conversions with a Unique URL

Conversion rates speak directly to the effectiveness of your donation page. For example, if 1,000 people visit your donation page, but only 10 visit your thank-you page, your conversion rate is only 1 percent. Houston, we have a problem (on the donation page).

One of the most reliable tools to track conversions is Google Analytics. Google Analytics has a feature called Goals that allows you to monitor your conversion rate, and make sense of users who donate.

The most common type of goal in Google Analytics is a conversion—when someone completes a specific action on your website—for example, joining your email list or making a donation.

2. A Sincere Thank You (Of Course)

Beyond basic manners, sincere appreciation builds stronger donor relationships, and thus donor loyalty.

But just including the words "Thank You" on your thank-you page isn't enough. Sincerity is the key, and there's no better way to express sincerity than video.

ProTip: Video is easier to create than ever before. Stop making excuses for not using video to thank donors.

3. Reinforce the Impact They Just Made

An important rule of donor retention is making donors feel like they are integral to the story. You do this by weaving them into the narrative as the hero who feeds hungry children, gives clean water, stops injustice, and so forth.

After thanking your donor, immediately reinforce the impact they made. "You just fed a hungry child . . . ."

4. Surprise and Delight Your New Donor

Your thank-you page is also an opportunity to surprise and delight your donor.

Again, this is the time to set the tone for a remarkable relationship. You want them to remember how they FEEL each time they interact with your nonprofit.

5. Encourage Social Sharing of Your Fundraiser

When someone makes a donation to your nonprofit, you are top of mind. But only for a limited time.

If you've done everything right up until this point (thanking them, connecting them to the impact, surprising and delighting them), they will be primed for a follow-up action. This is precisely the moment to ask them to share.

Will these five tactics work for your nonprofit to improve donor retention? Hopefully. But you can't pay the bills with "hopefully." Test it. Improve it. Never take off your lab coat. Refine your thank-you page by split-testing:

- Your thank-you message
- Your impact message
- Your sharing message

Select one of these variations to test to see if it improves your post-conversion goal (sharing your campaign, liking your Facebook page, taking a survey, joining your email newsletter, etc.) A few simple split-tests will help you create thank-you pages that improve donor retention.

CHAPTER 15

Crafting the Perfect Thank-You Email

The very next thing new donors will experience after seeing your thank-you page is receiving your thank-you email. Let's make sure you get that right.

Donor thank-you emails act as an essential piece of your email marketing strategy that can build longer-lasting donor relationships.

However, crafting the perfect message, from the subject line to the P.S., is key to tapping into the full potential of those benefits.

If you're struggling with how to create thoughtful donor thank yous, below are six ways you can write an email that your nonprofit will be proud to send out:

1. Customize your email to make it personal.
2. Keep your email short and to the point.
3. Use a conversational tone.

4. Make a great first impression.

5. Let donors know where the money is going.

6. Don't ask for more money.

Let's go deeper into how these components come together to create meaningful thank you's.

1. Make Your Donor Thank Yous More Personal

First, you want to create an email that is tailored to the person you're sending it to. The more time you spend customizing your emails, the more appreciated donors will feel. Donors are expecting to receive a genuine thank-you message. After all, they did make a donation to help support your cause.

Include their name in the greeting.

Donors are savvy enough to recognize when they're reading a mass email. Personalizing the greeting shows that you're willing to put in a little extra effort.

Send your email to a real person from a real person. Send emails with a real person's name in the 'From' section. People are more likely to open an email sent from a person they like, know, and trust.

2. Keep Your Thank-You Messages Short and to the Point

Donors want to feel appreciated, so conveying your gratitude should be the focal point.

Break up the text into short, easy-to-read paragraphs. Crucial information should be emphasized for the reader to take away (and tell others). Formatting your thank-you this way allows donors to skim through the email and still retain key details from the important sections.

There are multiple ways you can use images and videos to enhance your emails. You can include pictures or videos of:

- Staff expressing their gratitude through banners or posters.
- Work in the community.
- The people, places, or animals you serve.
- Content like this will give donors a better understanding of how their donation leads to real, tangible results.

3. Use a Conversational Tone in Your Donor Thank You

Imagine that you're talking to the donor in person. How would you speak to them? You're probably going to avoid using stiff, complicated language.

You're more likely to talk *with* the donor, not *at* the donor when engaging them in conversation. You might even use incomplete sentences and hand gestures to get your point across. All the strategies you use when talking face-to-face can be translated in your writing to make your message feel friendlier.

To make your email sound more conversational, you can:

- Use "you" more often than "I" or "we."
- Avoid insider terms (like peer-to-peer fundraising) without explaining them first.
- Make use of short or incomplete sentences.
- Ask questions.
- Add punctuation—or emphasize (bold, underline, italic, etc.) words—to better convey your point.

4. Make a Great First Impression

If the subject doesn't grab the donor's attention, then there is a possibility that they may never open it. Ditch the predictable subject lines and go for something that stands out.

For example, instead of going for the traditional "Thank you for your gift," go with something more immediate and eye-catching like "You're a Hero!"

Grab the reader's attention in the first few sentences as well. It's one thing to get them to open your email—*now* they have to be motivated to read it.

5. Let Donors Know How Their Gift Will Be Used

Donors who feel comfortable about where their money is going will be more likely to donate again.

As much as you can, with your nonprofit's capacity, give donors a clear understanding of how their specific support contributes to the larger picture—and remember that *how* you convey the message is just as important as what you say.

Just stating the facts is not as effective as revealing those facts through storytelling. For example, if your nonprofit provides school supplies for children whose family can't afford to buy them, tell a story about one of your students (with their permission). That narrative will resonate with donors.

Step #6: Focus on the Donor Thank You

Never ask donors for more money in your thank-you emails. They literally just gave you money, right?

Rather than asking for more money, give them options so they can stay updated on your nonprofit. For example:

- Include links to your social media.
- Suggest they sign up for your newsletter.
- Remind donors of upcoming events.
- Give donors a point of contact so they can respond if they want to.

These are all ways nonprofits can stay in the minds of their donors.

Ultimately, donors want to know that you care. Thank-you emails are an easy, inexpensive way to show your gratitude. Before you send out your donor thank yous, make sure that your message is donor-centric and that you expressed your appreciation in a clear, impactful way.

CHAPTER 16

A CARE Interview with Julie Edwards

I've already mentioned the Humane Society of Northeast Georgia several times, so how about I let Executive Director Julie Edwards tell you more?

Julie Edwards joined the Humane Society of Northeast Georgia in 2010 as the director of development and marketing and was responsible for managing annual fundraising events and implementing strategies to promote the organization's mission, services, and outreach efforts. In November, 2014, she assumed the role of executive director, overseeing operations and strategies to deliver ethical and effective animal welfare services to the regional community while developing long-term support for the organization.

Here's my interview with her.

John: How important is appreciating donors in your organization?

Julie: Donor appreciation is the keystone of our fundraising efforts; however, it hasn't always been. Our "lightbulb" moment happened in 2017 when our development team attended Cause Camp, our first-ever nonprofit conference, and saw you and other gurus like Tom Ahern and learned about "Donor Love." Since that time, we have consistently worked to define, implement and refine our stewardship strategies as well as learn as much as we can about effective donor relations.

John: Tell me about your process of thanking donors.

Julie: Our donor appreciation and stewardship strategies start before supporters ever give their first gift. We have implemented the "donor cycle" of "ask-thank-report" across all of our forms of giving, including online, social and direct mail. We want people who are familiar with our organization to see that we are using donor gifts to create the biggest impact for the cause and, in turn, feel compelled to give to support the mission.

We currently have three team members who work on donor relations—myself, our development director, and our development coordinator. Each of us has specific donor groups we steward—online, direct mail, major, midlevel, corporate, in-kind, recurring, etc. Donor relations are ongoing, day in and day out—a constant part of our fundraising strategy.

John: How does it differ with each relationship?

Julie: Donor relations differ by type (online, direct mail, major, midlevel, corporate, in-kind, recurring, first-time, tribute, etc.) and amount. For example, all first time and recurring donors receive a three-step thank you either by mail or email (depending on their method of giving). Donors who give $100 or more (online or offline) receive a handwritten card/note. Donors who give $1,000 or more receive a call from a board member.

For the past two years, we've hosted a thank-a-thon in October where all donors who gave in the past 18 months receive a call from the board, a personal letter from the executive director or postcard hand-signed by the team depending on their level of giving. Last year, we sent a small, inexpensive but meaningful holiday gift to all mid-level and major donors and plan to repeat it again this year. We also implemented donor newsletters last year and upped the frequency to four (one per quarter) this year as part of our "report" cycle.

In the past year, we also began using a video service (Bomb-Bomb) to send quick videos to donors to thank them, usually tied to a specific campaign or giving holiday.

John: What about your story tours? How do you decide to bring a donor on a story tour?

Julie: We have found it very challenging to get donors to visit our facility. Quite a few tell us it's just too sad and they don't want to see animals in "cages." Any donor is welcome on a tour and are taken on a tour modeled after Tammy Zonker's advice from the Nonprofit Storytelling Conference. First is a stop at our "wall of saves" in our Adoption Center, a wall of approximately 16 photos of some of our most compelling rescue cases where we will tell the story of 3-4 of the rescues and how they were helped by donors.

We then walk through the adoption rooms, pointing out various additions donors helped with—cat portals, sound system, etc.—and what the additions have meant for the health and wellbeing of our rescues. Next is the surgery suite where we talk about our low-cost spay/neuter services and their lifesaving impact and how donors help fund the service. The final stop is our Healthy Pet Clinic, again where we discuss the impact of offering low-cost basic veterinary services and how donors support this service. Most donors don't realize the depth and breadth of the services we provide so it's always an impactful journey.

John: For nonprofits who aren't yet appreciating their donors, what would be your number one piece of advice?

Julie: Start today! And an acknowledgment letter is not a thank-you letter. It can be time-consuming but develop a strategy. Start small and keep adding to your strategy as you grow. First steps could be as simple as carving out a few hours a week to make phone calls or making a short video showing an impactful mission moment on your phone and sending it via email with a thoughtful message (Look what you made happen!). There are many small, cost-effective/no-cost options for thanking your donors that don't take a lot of time that can make a big impact.

John: How does your executive staff and board nurture a culture of appreciation throughout the organization?

Julie: Our organization is still new to nurturing a culture of appreciation, but we made some great strides this fall. Our board actively participated in our Thank-A-Thon, making calls and signing postcards. We also are doing training on stewardship with our board and sharing "mission moments" at each board meeting. We also are nurturing a general culture of appreciation throughout our organization by defining and encouraging living out our goals as an organization.

Use my interview with Julie as inspiration to develop your own action plan to appreciate donors. As Julie advises, "Start today!" You'll stay in the hearts and minds of your donors for years to come.

PART FOUR

REPLY

Introduction

I have a morning ritual that's also a guilty pleasure: Reading love letters by Meredith Goldstein in the *Boston Globe*. Toast with almond butter, smoked salmon, black coffee, and Meredith. I'm a creature of habit. But I love this habit, because it's often the first thing that starts my day off with a laugh. (Relationships are human and therefore comedic).

Readers share serious problems ranging from young parents wondering what to do with overbearing grandparents, parents who lack boundaries, to how long should you wait to have sex. It provides informative nourishment—along with the smoked salmon.

But my favorite letters are what I call the "no reply." This is when someone went on a couple of dates that seemed to go well, but now the other person isn't responding at all. No reply. No texts, no Snapchats, no Instagram. Radio silence. It's also known as ghosting.

I laugh because I've been there. I think we've all been there. Meeting that special someone—or so we thought. And then nothing.

I was married. We had a wonderful child together. Then we got divorced, amicably.

By that time, there was match.com. I hadn't been on the dating scene for at least ten years, so I certainly didn't feel confident.

I had many pleasant exchanges. But eventually the other person would lose interest. Still, I learned to not take it personally. I learned to see the comedy in it. The "no reply" eventually had me laughing!

Then, one day, I sent a message. "What kind of dog do you wanna be when you grow up?"

Kate replied. We've been together ever since.

Let's look at where *your* replies to donors can lead your nonprofit.

CHAPTER 17

Why Your Donors Always Deserve a Reply

When I originally came up with the idea for this book, I struggled with the word "reply."

Sometimes I thought *respond* was the better word, simply because donors want you to respond to their sincerity, to their comments, to their replies to your emails, to your Facebook messages. They expect it. Eventually I landed on *reply*, because that is more to the point of this book: creating relationships with donors based on the spirit of dialogue.

As a kid, even in middle school, some of us learned the diagram of communication: Sender, receiver, message, feedback. You can't have real communications without feedback. And that's the reply! Reply says, "If I've heard you correctly, what you're saying is . . . . " These are basic "people skills" that many of us learned in couples therapy. I know I did!

This third part of CARE is all about making your donors feel heard and getting feedback from them as well so that you know you've heard them correctly. Naturally, as you continue this process, a relationship is developed. Trust grows. Donors come to like, know, and trust you simply because they know that they'll be heard and their voices matter. Any fundraising expert will tell you that feeling heard and feeling like you matter helps develop donor loyalty. Again, we're talking about relationships here.

Build a Responsive Marketing Funnel Donors Will Love

A marketing funnel is a framework to define the steps a supporter takes to go from awareness about your cause, to donating to your cause, to sharing your cause with friends.

But a marketing funnel isn't just a nice idea. In practice, it's a series of traffic sources, landing pages, and emails that work together to:

1. Capture interest—Once someone is interested in your cause, capture it.
2. Nurture interest—Build arousal through personalized and responsive email messages.
3. Convert interest—Maximize giving at the right moment.
4. Partner—Turn new supporters into spokespeople. Some are added to the development funnel.

Let's break down each of these stages and how you are constantly replying to your donors throughout.

Top of the Marketing Funnel: Capture Interest

Once someone is interested in your cause, capture it. And by capture, I mean emails.

For example, let's say a Facebook friend shares a petition to save the polar bears. If you aren't interested, you'll simply ignore it. But if you love polar bears, you will sign that petition (name, email, etc).

Polar Bears International captures your email, but they also capture:

- Your interest—In polar bears and other cuddly creatures.
- Your past support—In previous campaigns and fundraisers.
- Your permission—To send you emails about the polar bear campaign.
- Your news feed—Targeting you with Facebook ads about polar bears.
- Your future support—Volunteering, donating, and sharing campaigns.

The critical part of capturing interest (and emails) is this: You must offer enough value for them to give you their email so you can reply.

What kind of offers provide value?

- Free resources like toolkits, guides or ebooks.
- A discount on membership or event registration.
- Free invites to educational webinars.
- Action alerts and volunteer opportunities.
- Your amazing newsletter delivered via email.
- Photo contests, sweepstakes, and giveaways.

Regardless of your strategy, you must exchange value for value.

There is no value at all in filling out web forms. What do they get in reply when they complete your form?

Middle of the Marketing Funnel: Nurture Interest

Once someone has joined your list, they've raised their hand. They're saying "I want more." They're ripe for the asking. Your job is to offer compelling reasons to do more.

Email plays a critical role during the nurture phase. Only email allows you to send the right message, to the right people, at the right time:

- The right message—For each acquisition campaign, write a series of email messages designed to nurture interest and to deepen action. The key here is that the messages have to be relevant to the campaign.

- The right people—Before you start capturing emails, make sure you're properly segmenting contacts as they join your list. Capturing each contact's activity and interest allows you to nurture interest with relevant follow-up messages.

- The right time—When someone signs your petition, joins your newsletter, etc., they've expressed interest. You are on their mind. But not for long.

If you've done a good job in your follow-up emails, prospects won't need much convincing to take that next step.

Money in the Marketing Funnel: Convert Interest

Let's face it, when someone visits your donation page, it's an extremely rare and precious moment. ("OMG they actually clicked on our email and went to our donation page!")

It's a moment you can't afford NOT to seize!

Several factors increase the likelihood that someone will support your fundraiser:

- Audience relevance—Who's being asked to give? For example, people who signed the polar bear petition.
- Message relevance—Does the ask align with the audience? Your gift will save even more polar bears.
- Timing—When are they being asked? Recent polar bear petition signers are primed for giving.
- Feels—How amped up are they, emotionally? Unless they feel some love for the polar bears, very few will give money.

Here are some ways to encourage a gift on your website:

- Be sure to tell an impact story. Use one powerful picture that reinforces the story.
- Make the potential donor the hero. Talk about the impact they will make, and remove your organization from the narrative.
- Get rid of the word "DONATE" on your donate button. Instead, use language that communicates impact: "Feed Hungry Families." "Stop Hate in Your State." "Give Clean Water."
- Remove the sidebar and other distractions. You want your prospective donor to stay focused on completing the gift.
- Make sure your donation page is optimized for mobile.

Sharing in the Marketing Funnel: Turning Supporters into Spokespeople

The last part of the funnel is partnering, which can mean a number of things. But for new donors it will mean sharing your campaign. To facilitate sharing, add social media sharing features to your thank-you page. This way, donors are prompted to share immediately after giving.

The Marketing Vortex–A Disclaimer

One shortcoming of marketing funnels is what they suggest: Supporter actions are linear (awareness -> capture -> nurture -> convert).

But this couldn't be further from the truth. In reality, supporters enter and leave your funnel at various stages, making the funnel look more like a vortex. For example, many petition signers don't donate (i.e., convert), but instead share your campaign with their friends. Also, people in your email nurture sequence will continue to engage with social media and other messages at the top of the funnel.

Once you've created your donation page, thank-you page, and email nurture sequence, you can let the process run on its own. Your job now is to focus on driving relevant visitors to the top of the funnel (i.e., capture).

Lastly, make sure you monitor the effectiveness of your promotion, and the conversion rates of your emails and landing pages.

CHAPTER 18

The Gold Mine in Donor Surveys

The executive director of the small nonprofit hired me to help rework their donor communications and shift it from primarily organization-centric to donor-centric. The organization focused on alopecia, specifically supporting women with alopecia, as well as trying to end its stigma.

Even the executive director admitted they were bragging a little too much about the organization and not enough about the donors.

After talking to a few donors, I went back to the executive director and asked her again if there was any data that had been collected about donors over the past few years.

"Well, there is this spreadsheet we download each month (with a separate tab for each month)." In it, they had what you would expect: donor name, address, amounts given, dates given, and other standard data you'd expect from a donor database.

But there was one column, a custom field of donors answering a simple question: "What made you decide to give today?" When I saw this I nearly fell off my chair. I said to the executive director, "This is a gold mind!"

"How did you collect this data?" I asked

"Oh, that's a question we ask on our website every time someone makes a donation. We ask it on the thank-you page donors see immediately after giving," she said.

"What have you been doing with this data?" I asked.

"To be honest with you, we haven't really known how to use this information, we just think it's an important question to ask," she said.

After studying the answers, we began to see patterns. Specifically the reasons why people supported the organization. Some of these reasons were a surprise to the organization. For example, many women gave because they were looking for a cure, although there is currently no cure for alopecia. Others were looking for a group of empowered women who would not be defined by hair loss. Still others were looking for fashion advice. But for everyone, it was something personal. It was their story.

There are three great things about this kind of data.

First, when your donors feel like their story matters, it immediately creates trust, goodwill, and a deeper connection than if a question like this was never asked. When donors are asked why they give, they feel like their story matters.

Second, your donors' words are gospel. All too often, nonprofits like to use their own words to fundraise, as in "Our executive director says it best." Or, someone on the board with a creative writing degree thinks that they're clever enough to write something that will appeal directly to donors' hearts. But nothing can beat the language of the people. The words that your donors use are the words that you need to use when connecting with them, when appreciating them, when replying to them, and when encouraging them.

Third, it provides a powerful way to ask for another gift. Imagine if you were a donor who made a gift to an organization and a few weeks later you received an email encouraging you to join the monthly giving program. The email says that they're not asking everyone, just people like you who care. They go on to remind you what you said when you made your first gift. These are your words. How could you possibly be offended by them? Instead, it's likely you'll be reminded why you supported this organization in the first place, and you'll probably admire them for their savvy fundraising tactic.

In the end, this organization went on to use this information from the survey to improve their messaging, be much more donor-centric, and are well on their way to growing a community of loyal donors.

Was Everything to Your Liking?

Alice absolutely hated me. She was the head cook at a restaurant where I worked in the early 90s in Cambridge, Massachusetts. I don't know how I got a job as a waiter because I had absolutely no experience. And Alice knew it.

From day one, under the daze and confusion of my first few weeks and months, I would often take the wrong order from the kitchen—or even worse, take another waiter's order (a cardinal sin). If there wasn't the stainless steel service station that separated us, I swear she would've lunged at me with a butcher knife.

I was determined to become the best waiter. And eventually, I did. But it took three years. Along the way, I learned a lot, but one of the most important lessons I learned was a little trick from a fellow waiter, Lauri. She taught me to increase tip amounts and customer loyalty. Her trick was to ask a simple question at the end of each meal, sincerely and with complete vulnerability. The question: "Was everything to your liking?"

This question seemed to improve the temperament of customers, no matter if they were happy or not. It made them feel that they were eating at a very classy establishment. Also, it was a chance for them to either reinforce the wonderful decision that they made, or give feedback about their experience. If they didn't like a particular dish, I immediately scratched it off the order and they didn't have to pay for it, which they loved. If they liked everything about the meal, this question made them feel even better about their decision. Either way, when I asked this question, I noticed that because of the increased loyalty, trust, and goodwill, my tips increased as well.

Your donors are no different. Like customers in a restaurant, if you ask them how their experience was, they have a chance to give feedback, thus enhancing the relationship.

In *Retention Fundraising*, Roger Craver writes, "The loss of donors is silent and deadly. There's no screaming or shouting. No doors slamming. Seldom any advance notice. One day they're just gone." He goes on to reinforce the point that understanding donor motivations, which includes donor surveys, is absolutely critical to improve donor happiness and thus retention rates.

Top Tips and Mistakes to Avoid with Your Surveys

Surveys can accomplish many goals, but it's important to pick one primary goal and to be very clear about it in your survey strategy.

I worked with organizations that used surveys to achieve a number of goals:

1. To find new volunteers
2. To re-engage past donors
3. To learn what motivates your donors
4. To improve fundraising messaging
5. To learn more about their commitment to your organization and the cause

How will this survey data improve donor happiness? When you ask donors to take a survey, you're asking a lot. You're asking for their time, their focus, and their investment in your organization. You're asking for a certain level of commitment. But what will they get in return? Remember, you're developing a relationship with donors. If they invest in you, you have to invest in them. That's how relationships work.

If, on the other hand, your survey is clearly all about collecting data that will benefit your organization, donors will see right through that. They'll know it's not about them or the cause, so why would they invest their time in your survey?

Some reasons why donors would want to complete a survey include:

1. An interest in the topic.
2. They want to influence the organization.
3. They want to be heard.

Also think about how you will conduct the survey and where the data will live. The last thing you want to do is invest in yet another tool that requires a monthly fee. Review the types of survey questions you want to ask and see if there's a way to add these fields to your existing system of record, such as your fundraising software or donor database. Get the software companies support involved to help you understand how a survey can be easily created with existing features. That's their job, that's what they get paid for. And, believe me, they do not want to lose a customer!

Think about timing as well. Survey questions will be more likely to be answered if the donor expects the survey or at least isn't surprised by it. For example, asking them "What made you decide to give today?" immediately after they donated make sense, especially if they can answer this question quickly on the thank-you page. Additionally, they might always receive an email immediately, thanking them for their gift and asking them, "What made you decide to give today?" Obviously you'd have to do some thinking about which segments would be most appropriate for this question. For example, you might ask a first-time donor versus a donor who has given multiple times. A donor who has given multiple times might be a perfect fit for a donor commitment survey.

Bloomerang shared a great example of a donor commitment survey:

Please rank the following statements on a scale from 0-7, with 7 being agree the most:

I care passionately about the work of (organization's name).
0 1 2 3 4 5 6 7

My relationship with (organization's name) is something that I am very committed to.
0 1 2 3 4 5 6 7

My relationship with (organization's name) is very important to me.
0 1 2 3 4 5 6 7

(organization's name) is working to achieve a goal that I care passionately about.

0 1 2 3 4 5 6 7

In terms of other times you can survey donors, there are many. Registering for an event, signing up as a volunteer, downloading some helpful information from the website—you get the idea. If you ask these questions strategically, based on when the donor is interacting with your organization on their initiative, you're more likely to get quality data.

Respect Your Donors' Time

When considering the number of questions and the type of questions asked, less is more. Do your best to keep the survey donor-centric. This means appreciating their time and their effort, and not wasting it.

Never ever ask a survey question where you should already know the answer. For example, don't ask someone if they are a donor or how much they just gave. Questions like these can make your organization look completely clueless and might even infuriate some of your donors.

Keep the survey as short as possible and use language that is very simple; sixth grade reading level is best. The less language you can use and the more specific your questions are, the better the response rate. Additionally, make sure your survey renders on a smart phone in a way that's very user-friendly and doesn't require a lot of scrolling.

Take Action with the Data

Survey results shouldn't be left in a binder on a shelf. Even before you plan the survey, decide how you're going to take action on the results. Donors will expect this. It's part of the implied next step of taking a survey in the first place. "You asked me this question, I answered it, now what are you going to do about what I just said?"

Should someone express dissatisfaction in your survey, follow up quickly and sincerely to resolve whatever issues came up.

Just Get the Colonoscopy

During my work with Fight Colorectal Cancer (Fight CRC), I learned something that I kind of already knew. Men are afraid of getting colonoscopies. But I also learned that many men who have colon cancer regret not getting a colonoscopy earlier. They feel that if they had just gotten the colonoscopy, they may have caught the cancer in an earlier stage and wouldn't have had to deal with all the complications that advanced colon cancer brings with it.

Donor surveys are like getting a colonoscopy. It might feel scary at first, and it may even hurt a bit, but the information gained can save your nonprofit's life. Turning a blind eye, and not doing donor surveys because you're afraid of what donors might say, is essentially like letting cancer grow throughout your organization. That cancer is dissatisfaction, mistrust, and high attrition rates. Of course, many donors will love what you do, and those responses are certainly wonderful. But you also want to know about donors who aren't happy so that you can improve donor loyalty and retention rates.

You may be thinking, "We already know the five or six donors who aren't happy. They're just negative people, and no matter what we do, they'll always complain." The mistake you're making is this: if you know about five or six people that are complaining about your organization, how many others are dissatisfied but aren't saying a single word to you? This is precisely why you want to lean into a donor survey and embrace and appreciate whatever feedback you get.

Don't wait. Surveying donors and acting on their feedback is one of the most powerful ways to improve donor retention in the short term.

CHAPTER 19

Replying to Donors on Social Media

Do we have to reply to every single social media comment?

I've been asked this question countless times: at conferences, during webinars, and from clients.

Imagine you saw a story on social media from a nonprofit you supported as a monthly donor. Because the cause is so near and dear to you, you naturally share your story in the comments. Inspired, people would reply sharing their own story in turn. But not a single word from the organization that you thought earned your loyalty. Your monthly loyalty. Crickets.

How would you feel? Rejected? Confused? Neutral?

But you soon notice that the organization doesn't reply to most people who post to their page. You may no longer take their "no-reply" personally anymore, but their absence certainly hasn't enhanced your relationship. A no-reply can cause donors remorse, and at the very least, it's a lost opportunity to build trust with your community.

By the way, let's remember they were talking about replying to comments on social media. Thirty years ago, we had to make much more effort to respond to donors to build those relationships. Or maybe we've forgotten that responding to donors is a cause to enhance a relationship. Or maybe we feel that responding to a donor's comment is obligatory. Like connecting and appreciating, replying is always a cause and a wonderful opportunity to develop the donor relationship.

This question about whether you have to reply or not can also be a symptom of chronic CARElessness. In a CAREless organization, the donor is not at the center of communications. And this inevitably reflects in poor retention.

According to Roger Craver and many others, a key factor that influences donor loyalty is being heard. In fact, out of his seven key drivers on donor commitment, at least three play out on social media:

- Donors receive timely thank you.
- Donors receive opportunities to make their views known.
- Donors feel their involvement is appreciated.

We all know this stuff! It's Communications 101. You always enhance relationships when you create a space to make the other feel heard, to have a voice, to give feedback, to learn and to grow within the community.

The point here is that it's not about replying to every single comment on social media. That's not the point. The cure is leadership that supports CARE and a strategy that makes every effort to respond to as many comments as possible with a deep sense of appreciation.

If your social media strategy has donor happiness at the very center, replying to comments will be a core part of that strategy. You aren't just posting content and walking away. That's not dialogue. Dialogue, which is what grows a community (dialogue with your nonprofit and others in the community) means responding to people comments, recommendations, and stories.

Lastly, when you consistently appreciate and respond to comments, it instantly separates you from the majority of nonprofits who only offer crickets to their precious communities.

Why Donors Share on Social Media in the First Place

It seems that most brands don't understand why people really share on social media. Yes, people use social media for entertainment, to connect with others, and to be heard. But there's a deeper motivation behind why people share anything on social media.

People use social media to shore up their public persona—the version of themselves they want the world to see. Every single time we share something on social media, we are expressing who we are to friends, family, colleagues, and even complete strangers. And what we share reflects how we want to appear (our public self or persona). How peers perceive us is very important (we're hard-wired this way, sorry) and this plays out in what (and how) we share online. Most people won't admit this, but it's true.

Carl Jung talked about this persona as a "mask, designed on the one hand to make a definite impression upon others, and on the other to conceal the true nature of the individual."

So the next time you're crafting content, ask yourself, "What will their friends think about them when they share this post?"

It's one of the most important content marketing questions you can ask yourself.

The Six Personas of Social Media Sharing

If you've been using social media for a while, you've probably noticed that people connect and share information in different ways. Some of your friends share everything with everyone, and others are extremely selective about how (and what) they share.

The New York Times partnered with Latitude Research to conduct a study to understand why people share content. By conducting in-person interviews and sharing panels and surveying over 2,500 participants, they defined six sharing personas:

Altruists—These reliable folks want to be helpful and aspire to be seen as such. They primarily use Facebook and email.

Careerists—These well-educated folks seek to enhance their reputation by bringing professional (No LOLCats) value to their networks. They primarily use LinkedIn and email.

Hipsters—Hipsters share "hip" and creative content and view sharing as an integral part of their identity. They primarily use Facebook and Twitter.

Boomerangs—Boomerangs seek validation in the form of reactions to provocative content they share, even when it's negative responses. They primarily use Facebook, Twitter, and blogs.

Connectors—Connectors share to stay connected with friends, and make plans around the content they share. They primarily use Facebook and email in thoughtful but relaxed ways.

Selectives—These folks are extremely thoughtful and selective about what and with whom they share information, and assume that their friends will appreciate their resourcefulness. They primarily use email.

Give these personas some thought when you are creating both your own social media content strategy, as well as when you are replying to donors online.

CHAPTER 20

How Replies Grow Your Community

The Big Year with Steve Martin and Jack Black taught me one thing: Birders are obsessed with two things. Talking about birds and taking pictures of birds. Heck, I'm sure there's been more than a few fist fights over identifying birds. "No, you idiot, it's a red-throated... ." Comedic gold!

Nowhere else can passions play out more than on the Cornell Lab of Ornithology Facebook Page. Birders share photos of birds, and then good-naturedly argue about what type of bird it is! Most of their Facebook Page updates receive 25-50 comments or more in the first hour!

Take a page from Cornell Lab of Ornithology and be a conversation starter. Rather than posting content and then moving on to the next thing and saying, "Well, hey. Here's information about our event," seek a conversation. Again, social media is social, right?

Go back to the model of sender, receiver, message, and feedback.

Sender: You're the publisher of a post.

Receiver: Your fans see that post.

Message: The post itself.

Feedback: How your fans feel about your post.

The feedback is what too many organizations skip. But without it, communication doesn't happen. There is no dialogue without feedback.

Donors and supporters have questions, solutions, stories they can share with other people in the community. So instead of posting and walking away, publish updates that get people talking! Ask questions, ask for stories, ask for their opinions. Ask for help. Hey, here's what we found out. We have some questions from supporters and they have this issue. What do you guys think? What's your solution? Here's what we think, but what's your solution? What's your answer to this problem?

Underneath everything, of course, you seek an opportunity to understand your supporters and what they care about. You become a conversation starter, which adds tremendous value to the relationship you have with donors.

Be an Orchestra Conductor with Your Communications Channels

We have so many different channels that we use to communicate with our supporters. But too often we think of all these channels as separate. We have email over here, and we have Facebook and Twitter over there. I've seen many nonprofits isolate their communications channels from each other.

The most effective organizations approach their channels as a conductor. We want the channels to work in unity, or to play together like the instruments in an orchestra. One really great tool that I recommend to a lot of my clients is a content calendar or an editorial calendar where you're putting your major marque events on the calendar and then you're working all of your communication strategies around those events.

How do you get people interested? How do you get them talking about this event with their friends? How do you put call-to-actions out there? And how do you get your current people who have registered for that event to talk to their friends?

This is really part of your orchestration and your editorial calendar becomes the sheet music. You can drop in the messaging that makes sense throughout the month, and the following month and so forth. Your supporters will love you for this because your communications will sound like great music! They don't want to hear noise, and noise is what the average nonprofit puts out there.

The norm is to approach social media and content by flying by the seat of your pants. And the result is, unfortunately, noise. It's a lot of chatter. It's a lot of confusion for your supporters, donors, and volunteers. And it's really not that useful in the end.

It's much better to have an overarching story and see yourself as a conductor that's using multiple channels to embrace your donor and to produce music that they're going to love. That's what they want to hear.

Dealing with Haters and Lovers in Your Thriving Community

On the way to building your thriving community, you will have people who won't see things your way. Some will respectfully disagree with your point of view, some will misunderstand where you're coming from, and others are just gonna hate.

So what is a hater? Here's what the Urban Dictionary says:

A person that simply cannot be happy for another person's success. So rather than be happy they make a point of exposing a flaw in that person.

As a nonprofit marketer, you are tasked with growing a community of dedicated supporters, while also creating a safe and respectful place for discussion. Therefore, as a community manager, you must have a plan for haters.

Here's my five-phase plan for managing haters.

1. Have Rules for Haters

Set expectations for the community by stating clearly what's OK and what's not OK. Your rules (aka social media commenting policy) should have three components:

- Set the tone—Encourage lively discussion and invite a variety of differing opinions.
- Set expectations—Clearly define the line that must not be crossed.
- Consequences—People who repeatedly cross the line will be banned from posting comments.

A clear social media comment policy sets ground rules for your community while also helping moderators know when to delete comments or ban users.

2. Block Hater Comments

Protect your community from sticks and stones that haters like to throw.

Black, Jewish, LGBTQ+, disability communities, and many other groups are all-too familiar with hate speech. Set up filters to block hateful or hurtful language from appearing in the first place!

For example, Facebook allows you to block hateful language in your Page settings.

If one of these words is used in a post or comment, it will not appear on your Page.

3. Ban Haters

Many haters are repeat offenders. They feel better about themselves by making your nonprofit the bad guy. Your rules should include a clear policy for banning repeat offenders. The Humane Society clearly states theirs on Facebook: "If you repeatedly violate this policy, you will be removed from our page."

You can block haters on Twitter by selecting "Block" in the user actions on their profile.

You can ban haters on Facebook by selecting "Ban" after hiding their comment.

4. Let Your Community Deal with Haters

Trust your community to moderate themselves. They will often deal with haters in strict but respectful ways. Their responses to haters can range from simply correcting a fact, or taking part in a lively discussion. When this happens, let your community take the lead. Your community is far more effective at changing minds (or at least defending your nonprofit) than you are.

5. Turn Haters into Lovers

Or at least into likers.

Someone respectfully offering constructive criticism is not a hater. In many cases, they care as much as you do about the cause, but they have a different opinion. If you shut down respectful criticism instead of engaging in constructive dialogue, you could turn those people into haters. Instead, use your wisdom to:

- Take a breath and come from a positive position.
- Actively listen to those who respectfully disagree.
- Express appreciation for their comments.
- Seek to understand their position.
- Quickly take action to correct or resolve the issue, if needed.

Often, feeling heard is enough to win them over, even though they still might disagree with you.

Take Replying Deeper with Facebook Reactions

Facebook gives people six ways to react to content. Smart marketers will refocus their strategies on these six core emotions, removing much of the guesswork around your personas, your messaging, and your content.

How so? Ask yourself these questions about your Facebook updates, blog posts, and really all of your content:

- Like—What will people like about this topic? What does liking a post mean, anyhow?
- Love—What do people love about your cause? Will people love this post, or just like it?
- Ha ha—What makes your community lol? What do they find entertaining?

- Wow—What is amazing about your cause? What stories blow people away?
- Sad—What stories make people sad?
- Angry—What gets them angry? What injustices does your nonprofit fight?

Share stories intended to generate these six specific reactions. Then measure, repeat, refine. And play the edge. Any reaction is better than Like, which is neutral and basically says, "I saw your post." Like doesn't mean they like it, just that they saw it.

CHAPTER 21

Community Building Takes Time, So Be Patient

It seems like human nature is to focus even more on short-term fixes in the face of a threat, like famine or preventing the demise of your small nonprofit. Only 10,000 years ago, what you and I worried about the most was getting dinner. And we had a lot fewer choices: otter or snapping turtle. We worried about that while also worrying about a sabertooth tiger in the neighborhood.

Today, we have a completely different set of worries and problems. Within the nonprofit communications world, you have marketing communications people scared to death their job will get outsourced to an agency. You have executives and directors blindsided on a monthly basis by technology that changes how their supporters communicate with each other, and with their organization. And like our ancestors 10,000 years ago, some of us are also thrust into survival mode, especially in times when money is thin.

But in survival mode, you dial up board members and large donors. You look into shifting around your finances. You call in favors. You don't tweet and you don't post updates on Facebook.

But social media and communities in general are like a farm where growing a healthy crop takes at least a year. The crop is your community—your donors, supporters and volunteers. And the fruits from this crop are money, support and time.

Often, your required investment is nothing more than listening to what people need. For example, the Museum of Fine Arts has a strategy to engage their fans by paying attention to what's important to their community and then replying to those needs by being useful, even if it means losing ticket sales in the short term. This was evident in their Facebook update on April 15, 2013, the day of the Boston Marathon bombings.

Expressing the shock, sadness, and heroism many of their patrons were no doubt feeling, they invited everyone to the museum—free for the entire day—to be with each other in comfort and peace.

What Farmers Know

The farmer knows that she can't have apples next week. She knows that apples take two to three years to get a good yield. And if she's in survival mode, she'll sell off a few horses and a tractor. But selling those things will hurt big time because the crop is her destination. And she needs horses and tractors to get there.

Farmers get up at 3:00 a.m. every single day, no matter what. They pull the weeds, fertilize the soil, plant the seed, and do it all over again the next day. Never once do they expect to reap a harvest in a single day. Never once do they complain about the thankless hours of sweat and tears they pour into the land.

They know that to expect even the smallest baby green tomato within a week would go against common sense! They understand that the workings of the sun and the moon and the rain and the soil are all governed by the strict laws of cause and effect.

Farmers also know about reaping and sowing. For you, sowing means listening to how people are talking about you, selecting the right people to manage your social media profiles, and encouraging your community to take deeper actions. The farmer rolls up her sleeves, gets down on her knees, pulls the weeds, and closely inspects each apple tree to learn what's working and what's not. Paying close attention to their community is what enabled the Museum of Fine Arts to act quickly yet compassionately.

All social media works this way. The time, the effort, the planning, and the hearts all go a long way in creating a vibrant online community.

How Long Will It Take?

While raising money might be an obvious short-term goal, understand that the real value of relationships is the fruit they bear in the long-term. Yes, there are quick tactics to leverage your social community now, but those results pale in comparison to the long-term effect of using social media wisely. And you could risk turning off people who are just getting to know you.

The fruits you're reaping right now were sown from the seeds you planted twelve months ago. The relationships you took the time to nurture a year ago are now becoming sources of consistent support for your organization.

Most fundraising experts agree that the reason relationship building takes so long is human nature. You are dealing with people who, for the most part, are adults with their own sense of free will. People who decide to support your cause for reasons you may never know. People who post photos of their lunch on Instagram, and watch goats yelling like humans on YouTube. You get the idea.

Beth Kanter, a professional mentor of mine, and co-author of *The Networked Nonprofit* and *Measuring the Networked Nonprofit*, also agrees that good results from social media takes a year or more, depending on how mature your organization is.

Beth defines four phases nonprofits go through on their way to becoming a networked nonprofit that utilizes social media.

Crawl: If your nonprofit isn't consistently using social media and lacks a plan, you are in the "crawl" phase. The first step here is to develop a communications strategy for everything-direct mail, email, web, events. Once you have a plan, start using social media as a way to listen to your community, and add value by being useful.

Walk: If your nonprofit is consistently using social media to listen to your community, but lack a formal plan, you are in the "walk" phase. This is the phase where you want to focus on developing an array of best practices that work for your nonprofit. But because your executive staff might be pushing back with the usual ROI arguments, it's best to focus on small, low-risk campaigns intended to prove the value and benefit of using social media.

Run: If your nonprofit is strategically using social media to engage your community, but haven't integrated into all of your communications channels, you are at the run stage. This is the phase where you start sowing social media within all of your communications plans, with other channels like email, direct mail, traditional PR, advertising, signage, and social media.

Fly: If your nonprofit has integrated social media into your overall communications strategy, you are at this stage.

Learning to Fly

Chances are, right now you're wondering how your organization can progress through these phases.

In *The Networked Nonprofit*, Beth Kanter and Alison Fine discuss how to become a nonprofit that is "simple, agile, and transparent." They compare *The Networked Nonprofit* to a sponge that clings to rock no matter how many times it's battered by waves, yet can still filter out nutrients as waves pass through it. In other words, your organization grows by making it easy for "outsiders to get in and insiders to get out."

There are several "farmer-like" qualities that networked nonprofits have:

Value networks—You value the connections your nonprofit has online and offline. And you nurture key relationships that help strengthen the network. Farmers value their relationships with grocery stores and customers.

Comfort with tools—Your nonprofit is comfortable using blogs, Twitter, Facebook, Instagram and other tools that facilitate two-way conversation. Farmers have always been comfortable with tools.

Networked ecosystem—You're not trying to do it all. Your nonprofit knows that it's part of a much larger ecosystem of organizations and individuals that are all incredible resources for their efforts. Farmers know that they can't grow a healthy crop without fertilizer, tractor parts, and gasoline.

Courageous—You're not afraid to lose control of your message, your logo, or your message. You know that the wisdom and passion of your supporters can have an infinitely greater impact than you and your staff. Heirloom tomatoes are so beautiful and tasty precisely because tomato farmers let tomatoes do what they naturally do.

Trusting—You trust your supporters to make good decisions on behalf of your organization. Your organization focuses on giving them the tools they need instead of enforcing copyright laws. A good farmer trusts everyone she works with, and in turn, those people work harder for the farm.

Athletic—Social media is not a set of tools to be used only by your IT or marketing folks. Your organization understands the power that social media has in the lives of your supporters because you use the tools yourself. It's a contact sport. Farmers have dirty hands. Enough said.

Developing these traits within your organization is the most important thing you can do to create long-term success with social media. And the best place to start is where you are, right now.

CHAPTER 22

A CARE Interview with Sasha Purpura

Sasha Purpura is the executive director of Food For Free (FFF), a nonprofit dedicated to providing everyone in Greater Boston with reliable access to nutritional food. Under her leadership, Food For Free has grown dramatically, tripling its fundraising, staff, and food rescue, while implementing multiple new programs and fostering partnerships with educational institutions throughout the region. She holds a BS in Computer Science from Boston University and received her MBA in organizational and environmental sustainability from Antioch University.

I interviewed Sasha about the ways her nonprofit replies to donors.

John: An important part of replying and responding to donors is reporting back about the impact of their gift. How does your nonprofit report back about impact to make donors feel like they matter?

Sasha: Our overall philosophy is that we need to be prompt with donors and, when telling them of the great work we're doing, always tie it back to their help—most often with a thank you.

Within a few days of receiving a gift, we send a customized receipt. In addition to thanking the donor, we include information on how their gift will impact the program or programs they're supporting. This includes the services we will be able to provide and how many people we'll reach. It is signed by the executive and development directors.

In certain cases, like a big gift, or a donor we're trying to cultivate, the executive director will also include a brief note or handwritten thank you on the receipt. When gifts are $200 or higher, the donor also receives a handwritten thank-you card from the development or executive director. For donors that give at least four times a year, we send an annual thank you, again, detailing the program impact they are supporting.

John: Describe your process for reporting back about impact to donors. Does it differ with gift size or number of gifts given?

Sasha: For our major donors and major donor prospects ($10,000 and above), we send a quarterly "Executive Director Update" letter providing more detailed updates on the organization including recent program impacts and future plans.

When this group of donors is amenable, the executive director schedules in-person coffee or meetings two to four times a year during which she shares more detail on the organization's activities, impacts, and plans and asks for feedback.

We try to have one event each year for this top-giving group. Two years in a row, we held an open house, inviting people to our offices to meet our staff and learn about our programs. We've also held two breakfasts where we covered the need we're addressing and highlighted some of the organizations we're serving.

John: How are you using email newsletters and social media to report back about the wonderful impact your donors have made?

Sasha: More generally, we send out a quarterly email newsletter to anyone on our mailing list. This includes specific program updates (e.g., new food donors, new recipient agencies, etc.), often a highlight of how our food is helping one of the agencies we serve, and general information about organizational changes. We don't always overtly state that this work is because of our donors, but believe this communication keeps them engaged and implicitly conveys the impact that they're having. Our annual report details the overall impact of all of our donors and lists all of our donors by name.

We take advantage of social media (Instagram, Facebook, and Twitter) to share real-time updates about our programs. The overall goal of our posts is to keep donors engaged in the work we're doing and feeling good about their contribution to that work. We always try to include pictures where allowable. We share stats on the need and how our programs are addressing that need, show volunteers at work, and share program impacts, both numbers and quotes from recipients. We often refer to the fact that this work would not be possible without the support of the community. During the giving season, we share a series of photos overwritten with a thank you and stats on the work that we're doing.

John: How have these strategies impacted your retention rates?

Sasha: We have above average retention rates. In fiscal year 2019, our overall retention rate was 57 percent versus an industry average of 45 percent. For repeat donors, we saw an above average rate of 73 percent versus the industry's 61 percent.

We attribute this retention rate to our responsiveness to and focus on donors. It is only over the past few years that we have made it a top priority to send a gift receipt and thank you within days of receiving the contribution. Additionally, our hand-written thank-you cards are mailed within two to four days of the gift. We believe this level of responsiveness builds loyalty from our donors. Many of our larger donors have shared with us that they very much appreciate the personal attention and that they often don't receive that from the organizations they support.

John: What other specific tips would you give to a nonprofit that currently has poor or declining retention rates?

Sasha: Our primary advice to other nonprofits in regards to donor cultivation and retention is "communication and appreciation." We have heard anecdotal stories from our donors of organizations that never sent a thank you or don't respond to questions either emailed or posted on social media. We feel that is the quickest way to lose support. Donors give because they care and, oftentimes, want to be a part of something. Showing appreciation—in a timely manner—and then engaging them in the work through communication, goes a long way in making them feel a part of the team. Always send a thank you, no matter how small the gift. Include, in that thank you, the work that that gift will enable. Consistently share impacts and stories on social media and communicate through other channels as well—newsletters, events, in person, etc.

PART FIVE

ENCOURAGE

Introduction

Having good friends is like being equipped with a powerful auxiliary engine. When we encounter a steep hill or an obstacle, we can encourage each other and find the strength to keep pressing forward.
—Daisaku Ikeda

It's a memory so burned in my brain it feels like yesterday every time I think of it. I was eight.

On a cold winter morning, December 22, 1974, my mom lay on my parent's bed with both arms outstretched towards the ceiling. Her arms were trembling and reaching upward towards the heavens but she was totally unconscious. My dad calmly collected his wallet and keys from his top dresser drawer.

The housekeeper whisked my two brothers and I into the kitchen and shut the door. We could see the gurney through the crack in the kitchen door as my mom was led down the hallway and into the awaiting ambulance. I was scared and confused. She was 40.

My mom had an "inoperable" brain aneurysm and needed surgery right away. From Waterbury hospital, she was transferred to Columbia Presbyterian New York on New Year's Eve. She had two brain surgeries, the first on January 2, 1975 for four and a half hours and the second on January 8, 1975 for eight and half hours.

After surgery, my mom was in a coma for a couple of weeks.

When my mom awoke after brain surgery, she was half paralyzed, almost completely blind, and had lost the ability to speak. She had no clue what was happening.

Seeing that she was desperate to say something, the nurses handed her a pad and pencil. My mom wrote, "Are my three boys OK?"

After some back and forth, she understood two things:

1. There was no car accident
2. She had a long road ahead of her

Doctors told her to prepare for life in a wheelchair, blindness, and limited ability to speak. Again, my mom scratched out on a piece of paper "I've got three boys to raise. Watch me. I will fully recover!"

Her recovery was encouraged by the village—her family, friends, neighbors, occupational therapists, and Eileen. Eileen was a swimming instructor my dad hired to work with my mom almost full-time.

Day in and day out, my mom struggled in the pool with Eileen by her side. "Come on Jean, you can do it! Just a few more feet, keep kicking. Kick, kick, kick!" I remember Eileen's encouragement as my mom struggled in the pool like it was yesterday.

Here are some milestones from her one-page diary:

February 18, 1975—Took first steps between parallel bars

March 6, 1975—Transferred to Waterbury Hospital

March 17, 1975—Transferred to Gaylord Rehab.

April 25, 1975—Transferred home. Hoorah! Came home in a wheelchair—able to do very little for myself and with only partial vision in each eye.

April 6, 1976—Swam length of pool

June 17, 1976—Swam 50 lengths of pool

At the end, she wrote, "I think I was called and put to the test to help other people in the same boat."

Proverbs 25:11 says, "A word fitly spoken is like apples of gold in settings of silver." How many times do we wish a dear one were with us so we could tell them how much we appreciated them when they were with us. Tell them now.

My mom lived a long, victorious, healthy life and eventually died in her sleep on July 18, 2002. You might think my mom was a walking, talking miracle. But she was not special. We all have unlimited potential to overcome impossible odds.

And your donors are no different. They want to encourage and want to be encouraged. Let's look at how you make that happen.

" DIARY OF A PATIENT "

Graduated by degrees from:

Waterbury Hospital
Columbia Presbyterian
Gaylord Rehabilitation Center
S.M. Spinster of Medicine
M.L. Master of Laughter
P.H.T. Pull Hard Together

December 22, 1974	-	Rushed to Waterbury Hospital Diagnosis: Inoperable - Aneurysm
December 31, 1974	-	Transferred to Columbia Presbyterian for Brain Operations
January 2, 1975	-	First Operation - 4 1/2 hours
January 8, 1975	-	Second Operation - 8 1/2 hours
February 18, 1975	-	Took first step between parallel bars
March 6, 1975	-	Transferred to Waterbury Hospital
March 17, 1975	-	Transferred to Gaylord Rehab.
April 25, 1975	-	Transferred home. Hoorah!
	-	Came home in a wheelchair - able to do very little for myself and with only partial vision in each eye.

Today - can read anything I want to, no wheelchair, can do anything I want around the house.

Took lessons for swimming for five months.

April 6, 1976	-	Swam length of pool
June 17, 1976	-	Swam 50 lengths of pool

Bill and I have a favorite in the Bible. Rom. 8:28 - "For all things happen for good to those who love God and are called according to His purposes." Now it's hard to see what good could happen when this tragedy hit our home, but it happened. One - it has made our family a lot closer, and has given us a great deal more understanding and compassion toward other people's troubles and anxieties. I think I was called and put to the test to help other people in the same boat.

Another - Prov. 25:11 "A word fitly spoken is like apples of gold in a setting of silver." Encourage each other. How many times do we wish a dear one were with us so we could tell them how much we appreciated them when they were with us. Tell them now. Don't take things lightly. Tragedy can strike anywhere and anytime. Make the most of each day. It's a gift from God!

CHAPTER 23

Create Journeys for Donors, Not Dead Ends

Henry Ford's Model T was regarded as the first affordable automobile that opened up a world of travel and adventure to the average Joe. Today, it remains on the top ten list of most sold cars of all time.

The Model T wasn't the first car, and it wasn't the only model Ford had. But, it was the first mass-produced car with interchangeable parts, making it extremely affordable to the middle class. If you wanted a car, the Model T was really the only smart and affordable choice. "I will build a motor car for the great multitude. It will be large enough for the family, but small enough for the individual to run and care for," said Ford.

Now, fast forward to today, where consumers expect brands to provide not just choices but a journey. To keep a customer for life, Ford supports each customer as they take their own journey from a college student (with help from mom and dad), to newly married, to the minivan family, to Mustang retirement.

Your nonprofit must also provide a path from college grads on a budget all the way to legacy-focused grandparents. How many options are you giving potential donors?

Isn't the essence of donor stewardship the journey you take together?

If you see your nonprofit in any of the following descriptions, you could be unknowingly creating not a journey, but a dead-end for your donors:

- We have one donation page for everyone, regardless of how much they've given, how many times they've given or how frequently they've given.
- We have one gift menu or array for everyone, regardless of how much they've given, how many times they've given or how frequently they've given.
- We have one email for everyone, regardless of how much they've given, how many times they've given or how frequently they've given.
- We have the same thank-you note for everyone, regardless of how much they've given, how many times they've given or how frequently they've given.

"She is not your donor. You are one of her charities."—Mark Phillips

Mark Phillips is a fundraising and development expert who manages Bluefrog Fundraising in the U.K..

In one simple and lucid statement, Mark dismantles a commonly held, unspoken myth that many nonprofit marketers and fundraisers unknowingly harbor: Their charity is the only charity their donors think about, dream about, pay attention to, and support. As you read this, you may be thinking, "Of course this isn't true! Of course we know our donors support other charities."

Still, let's make Mark's wisdom our mantra: "She is not your donor. You are one of her charities."

What's the Next Step for Your Donor?

The young man who rang the doorbell looked pleasant and harmless enough, so I opened the door. "Hi, I'm Michael with WGBH, Public TV," he said.

One summer during my college days, I did canvassing for an environmental organization. Not easy work. Cold calling, knocking on doors, hearing a lot of "no." Not too many doors were slammed in my face, but still, my close ratio was pretty low. I somehow couldn't get past the instinct to repel that exists in most of us when a stranger comes to our front door.

One day, my supervisor shared a trick for turning "No" into "Yes." He told me "Don't try to get people to say, 'Yes.' People are naturally more comfortable saying 'No' when they first meet a stranger, so try asking a question that will likely be answered with a 'No' when they actually mean 'Yes.'"

I was confused. "Here's the one I use," he said. "Is now a bad time?"

As if pulling from the same playbook, Michael at my door asked the same exact question: "Did I catch you at a bad time?"

"No," I replied.

This guy was good. Very good. He was also handsome, tall, and conveyed a youthful earnestness, which didn't hurt.

Michael proceeded to tell me that he was in the neighborhood visiting current members of WGBH. I remember donating once or twice in the past couple of years to support public television, but I wouldn't necessarily call myself a member. But he called me a member.

I looked at his clipboard, and he had a list of names of my neighbors, many of whom I knew. All WGBH supporters.

He said he was visiting WGBH members in my neighborhood in an effort to promote their new monthly giving program. He said there is no pressure to join on the spot, but he'd leave me with a brochure and application to join whenever it was convenient for me.

There are so many things WGBH did right in this campaign all in the interest of donor stewardship and in encouraging each member to take the next step. Let's break it down.

Their investment was appropriate for the return. Monthly giving has a 90 percent retention rate, so if members joined the program, they would likely give hundreds of dollars each year, possibly for several years. The investment of having boots on the ground, walking neighborhoods, is a smart investment. Face-to-face fundraising has the highest close rate. People are much more likely to join a monthly giving program if they are asked directly, face-to-face, compared to email or any other marketing channel.

Always Know What's Next

One of the biggest mistakes with donor communications is assuming your job is done after the fundraising transaction is complete. But after that first gift, most donors move on with their busy lives. Chances are, they won't remember your nonprofit if you don't stay in touch. And if they don't remember you, good luck retaining them!

A simple way to set the tone for an ongoing relationship is to consistently answer this question: What's next? It's your job to set expectations and tell donors what's next at each step in the relationship.

For example:

What about inviting new donors to share your most popular blog posts?

What about asking new donors to invite their friends? Direct appeals among friends often have the highest conversion rates.

What about asking event registrants to follow you on Instagram? What about asking petition signers to share pics with a campaign hashtag?

What about asking new donors to watch a YouTube video with a deeper story?

And what about people who attended that recent event? What's next for them?

The point is to always suggest a next step each time you engage with a donor. Whether it's watching a video or signing a petition, engaging subscribers is all about baby steps. A click is a little "yes" that often leads to big "YES."

The more your donor communications sets expectations and builds anticipation, the more likely supporters will stay with you for the long journey.

Who Should Go Down Which Path?

I am not a development expert and I am not a legacy gifts expert, far from it. So I will not address the complex and rich relationships that are better understood by those experts. However, I do know a bit about online giving and first-time donors, repeat donors, and monthly donors whose relationships are nurtured with digital communications (website, email, social, chats, marketing automation, etc.).

Let's discuss a path for each of these donor segments, keeping in mind what we know about them, their potential motivation in a relationship, and the next step for them in their journey.

People who gave once in the past year: The only thing we know about people who have given to you one time is that they are willing and able to part with their money. That's all we know about them. They may have been guilted into giving by a good intentioned friend, or maybe they saw breaking news about a tsunami and gave as an impulse gift. Other than that, we know nothing about their interest in our cause or even our nonprofit. The next step for them is to nurture whatever interest they might have and ask for another gift. And yes, it's OK to ask more than once.

People who gave twice in the past year: People who gave twice in the past year to your organization have demonstrated that they have gone beyond impulse giving. Two gifts demonstrate at least a remote interest in going on a journey with your nonprofit. People who have given twice in the past year are perfect candidates for your monthly giving program. And if they've given more than twice in the past year, it's like they are begging to join your monthly giving program.

People who give monthly: Members of your monthly giving program should be treated like gold. But don't be afraid to give them even more opportunities to support your cause, such as special gifts or upgrades to your annual appeal, etc. Monthly donors are more likely to support these types of appeals. You just have to ask. Remember, the fact that they have tried your monthly giving program is an expression of commitment to the wonderful work you're doing and commitment to the journey that you have both started together.

People who gave over a year ago: These people have moved on, or lost interest in the work you're doing. But maybe not. Maybe you've just done a poor job at communicating with them. The next step in their journey is to remember you, to be reminded of that time when they did have an interest in making an impact with your organization.

Your very first touch point shouldn't be a hard ask, obviously. Instead, thank them for their past support no matter how long ago it was. Thank them with no strings attached. Express appreciation for their past support. Of course, you can make an indirect ask at this time, but the important thing is to make the first bit of communication primarily one of appreciation. Finally, accept the reality that most of these people might be lost forever. Just move on.

People who haven't given yet but are on your email list: These people are on your email list for some reason. At some point there was an interest in your newsletter, a petition you offered, or a pledge that they signed. The next step for them might be responding to a very small ask, say five or ten dollars related in some way to their first interaction with you (if you know what that was). For example if they signed a pledge to end hunger, thank them for standing with others to fight hunger and offer a very small way for them to take that next step in ending hunger.

Hopefully, you have already segmented these groups of people in your database, and if so, kudos to you. If not, get with your fundraising software vendor, or fundraising and marketing consultant, to discuss how to segment these groups of people in your database.

This is really the first step to scaling the type of communication that offers a journey that is unique to each of these groups of people. The more you can offer a path that speaks to each person's journey, the more likely you will increase their loyalty to your organization.

You will still be one of many charities they support, but instead of being at the bottom of their list, you will now be in the top ten! Offering a CAREful journey to your donors will instantly separate you from a sea of charities who still mostly offer a dead end. And your donors will love you for it!

Chapter 24

Why Offering Monthly Giving is a Must

At the very beginning of this book, you learned the shocking truth about donor retention: Most nonprofits lose as many as 75 percent of their first-time donors.

You also learned how to improve donor retention rates using the CARE framework. You learned why it's essential to connect with the donors so that they feel a personal experience when they give. You learned the power of appreciation and how you really can't say thank you too much. You learned to give them an opportunity to be heard, to remind them of the impact they've made, and to respond to their sincerity.

Now, as you learn about encouraging your donors to take that next step, we absolutely must look at monthly giving as an essential next step for first-time and returning donors.

What's So Great about Monthly Giving?

The Blackbaud Institute's *Sustainers in Focus* reported that donation revenue has the potential to increase by a whopping 50-300 percent per donor when you can get them to commit to monthly giving.

There are at least seven excellent reasons why monthly giving should be a must for every nonprofit:

1. Monthly Giving Increases Donor Retention

Check out these frightening stats from the 2018 Fundraising Effectiveness Survey Report:

- Every 100 donors gained in 2017 was offset by 99 lost donors through attrition. Ouch!
- Every $100 gained in 2016 was offset by $95 in losses through gift attrition. Yikes!
- The most significant losses in donors came from lapsed new donors. Oh no!
- The 2018 Fundraising Effectiveness Survey Report also includes this very promising stat: Monthly donors have a 90 percent retention rate. 90 percent!

2. Monthly Giving Increases Lifetime Donor Value

Increasing lifetime donor value is a breeze when you have a 90 percent rate. Monthly donors give more often (every month) and they continue giving for many years.

3. Monthly Giving Creates Predictable Revenue for Your Organization

If you're like most fundraisers, you know how difficult it is to predict how much money you'll raise month-to-month. You might have a list of donors who said they'd give next month, but a promise is very different from a check. It's not money in the bank.

However, because monthly donors automatically get charged each month, predicting revenue over 3, 6, or even 12 months becomes so much easier!

4. Monthly Giving Lowers Fundraising Costs

I tell my clients that they shouldn't celebrate that new donor who gave $25. The reason? The cost of acquisition often exceeds the small donations first-time donors typically give.

With a 90 percent retention rate, the cost to retain recurring donors goes way down.

5. Monthly Giving Lets You Focus on Building Relationships

Most fundraisers admit that they don't like asking for money over and over again. It can turn what should be a rewarding relationship into an awkward relationship.

Recurring giving removes the constant asking from your relationship with donors and allows you to focus on building partnerships with these donors. Onward and upward!

6. Monthly Giving is Less Painful for Donors

NPR pitches monthly giving by telling listeners to "give less." Give less? Yes, give less now but give every month.

They're tapping into a deeply human tendency to defer immediate pain. Parting with $10 now is much less painful than parting with $120 now.

Less pain for the donor means that they'll be more likely to give now.

7. Monthly Giving is a Huge Convenience for Donors

Lastly, let's not forget the considerable convenience of recurring giving. After signing up, there's nothing they need to do except feel great about supporting their favorite cause every single month.

So how do you get started with monthly giving? Obviously, there are entire books dedicated to this topic. My personal must-read recommendation is *Monthly Giving—The Sleeping Giant: How Small Gifts Can Become Powerful Tools to Support any Organization* by Erica Waasdorp.

How to Create a Successful Monthly Giving Program

Monthly giving has been my personal passion with clients for years, and I've learned a lot about what works and what doesn't.

1. Own It.

The success or failure of your monthly giving program ultimately depends on having a single person who takes full responsibility for the program. Executive staff and board must get out of the way and completely support this person. Hire a consultant to support and guide that staff person if needed. The investment in training, education, strategy, etc. will pay for itself.

2. Know and Understand What Your Donors Want.

Don't guess what your donors want. Don't assume you know what they want. Your research should go well beyond, "Well, we are a lupus foundation, so of course our donors care about lupus and they're so passionate about it."

CARE means understanding your donors as dynamic human beings with countless struggles, interests, dreams, and preoccupations. Good research shows that people who are impacted by lupus (as an example) are also interested in eating healthy, exercising, and maybe other lupus-related issues.

Research your previous campaigns. Go through and look at any projects, programs, campaigns, and any big segments in your database, and then come up with ideas for your monthly giving program. For example, let's say your nonprofit does a huge fundraising campaign around an issue every year. It's on a specific topic and people love it. They give a lot each year and it's always a success. Maybe that's the angle you should use with your monthly giving program. Also, look at the emails that get the highest open rates and the stories in your email newsletter that get the most clicks.

All of this information will help you understand what people want.

3. Develop a Unique Brand for Your Program.

You want to brand your monthly giving program. You want your monthly giving program to be recognizable and differentiated from your main brand. This way if someone goes to your website just to make a donation, they interact with your main brand. But if they're going to become a monthly donor, you want it to feel different, because the psychology behind monthly giving centers around exclusivity.

You want to come up with a name that your monthly donors would want to call themselves, not something cute that you came up with at a board meeting.

If they're a member of your monthly giving program, they want to identify as a champion, a guardian, a defender, an agitator. Create a logo for your monthly giving program, but one that reflects your main logo.

4. Create a Separate Webpage for Your Monthly Giving Program.

This helps convey a sense of importance. Again, what's really behind becoming a monthly donor is this idea of exclusivity. Human beings are joiners. Whether you look at behavioral economics or human evolution, you'll find that one core piece of behavior, whether as a consumer or a donor: I'm in the group.

We love to quickly identify who we are in relation to other people. Becoming part of the group of monthly givers means I am not just a one-off donor. I'm special.

5. Give Them Something No One Else Gets.

Another way to trigger exclusivity is with content. If you're in a monthly giving program, you are getting this super special insider newsletter. There should be special access too—if we have a big, huge event coming up, monthly donors get special, red carpet treatment. Maybe you have a sponsor, such as a local retailer who could offer a members-only discount to your monthly donors.

6. Communicate Bite-Sized Impacts.

Give the sense that the donor, every single month, is making a very specific impact that ties back to that donation. Make it realistic in terms of what that dollar amount might mean to the donor.

For example, Investigator Allies are the monthly donors for Mercy for Animals. What do investigator allies do? Investigator allies help investigators expose unspeakable animal cruelty at factory farms. Allies are critical in helping these brave investigators.

"I'm stopping baby chicks from being ground up alive just for being born male." Pretty horrific stuff, and those monthly donors are putting a stop to it.

Other examples:

- Save an acre of rainforest each month for X dollars
- Provide legal defense for one immigrant each month
- Stock a classroom with school supplies each month

The more you equate the gift to its relative impact, the more the donor is going to keep coming back. They feel that made a meaningful and real impact that swells them with pride: "Look what I did!"

7. Communicate Program Benefits.

So when someone joins your monthly giving program, you want to tell them, "Hey, it's not just a one-way street. Yes, thank you for your donation, but here's all the stuff you're going to get in return." Again, reinforce the exclusivity.

8. Make Monthly Giving Your Default on Your Main Giving Page.

This tells all potential donors, first time or repeat, that this is the best way to support your organization. Of course, give them an option for a one-time gift, if they want to start there. But by offering monthly giving as the default, you send a signal of importance that says, "This is the best way to make an impact."

9. Keeping Up with the Joneses.

If you can, display the names of other donors or members of your monthly giving program. Donors will be more likely to give if they've seen that others have given first. The list of names is literally the group they will be joining, which is again one of the primary motivations for joining a monthly giving program—to be a member of an exclusive and special group of people who CARE.

Monthly giving is a great way to encourage your donors and you can't go wrong if you follow these tips.

CHAPTER 25

10 Mistakes That Discourage First-Time Donors

Any fundraiser will agree that keeping a first-time donor happy is cheaper than replacing that donor. In fact, attracting and acquiring a new donor is ten times more expensive than keeping an existing donor.

Even if you're not a math wiz, you can see that the surest way to positive net revenue is to prioritize retention over acquisition.

I've talked a lot throughout this book about encouraging your donors. Of course, if you do the wrong things, you'll *discourage* them. Now, I'll focus on mistakes nonprofits make that make donors leave.

1. Not Saying Thank You

It's the A in CARE and something your mother taught you, so hopefully you're already thanking donors. If not, you'll lose about 13 percent of your first-time donors, according to Bloomerang.

2. Bragging about Your Organization Instead of the Donor

If you're bragging to first-time donors about how great your organization is, you're doing it wrong. Supporters yearn for stories about people that are impacted by your cause. The against-all-odds cancer survivor, the tattered puppy who found her person—that's what you talk about, especially to new donors.

3. Not Personalizing Your Email Message with at Least Their First Name

When someone donates for the very first time (or any time for that matter), they give you their first name. Not using at least their first name to personalize your follow-up emails takes away from that great first impression you're trying to make.

4. Sending the Exact Same Fundraising Emails to All Donors

When you blast to your entire list with a fundraising email, you ignore each supporter's unique relationship with your organization. Of course, thoughtfully crafting an email for each and every donor won't scale. But you can craft messages for each major donor segment (first-time, repeat, monthly, etc.).

5. Subjecting the Donor to a Horrible Online Experience

If your website isn't mobile, or if you're using CAPTCHAS on your donation page, you are literally throwing money out the window. Not only that, you give potential donors a very good reason to support your competition.

6. Not Asking Donors Why They Gave

If you want to retain more donors, make sure you ask them the most important question. What made you decide to give your first gift?

You can ask this in-person, on your donation thank you page, or in a short follow-up survey. You can then use their words when asking them to give a second gift or better yet, become a recurring donor. Talk about a smart use of data!

7. Not Sharing Impact Stories

Donors give because they want to affirm their belief that they are the most important, VIP, human being. They want to change the world. Don't assume donors know the impact of their gift. Remind them again and again.

8. Not Asking for a Second Gift

Donors give because it makes them feel great. If you feel that asking for a second gift is too pushy, rethink your approach. It's just another way to encourage donors.

9. Not Telling the Donor What's Next

The more your donor communications set expectations and build anticipation, the more likely supporters will stay with you for the long journey. Each time a donor interacts with your organization, it's your job to tell them what's next and to encourage that next step in the relationship.

10. Not Fixing What's Broken with Your Donor Retention Strategy

You may not be making all the mistakes mentioned above, but chances are you're making at least one mistake. Regardless, you owe it to your donors to find out what's broken and fix it.

If you've made it this far in the book, I know you sincerely want to avoid these mistakes and do better by your donors. After all, they deserve to be treated with CARE.

CHAPTER 26

A CARE Interview with Frank Velásquez Jr.

Inspired to "dare greatly," Frank Velásquez Jr. leads and collaborates with passion, authenticity, and an open mind. A racial equity and social justice advocate, he connects to the stories that make each of us who we are and the stories that inextricably connect us to each other. A natural storyteller, he loves the task of bringing greater local, statewide, and national attention to poverty and inequity through JobPath's work, where he is the executive director.

I spoke with Frank about how JobPath encourages donors.

John: How do you encourage new donors to take the next step in commitment with your story tours? What's the process?

Frank: The purpose of JobPath's story tours is to provide potential donors (individuals, foundations, corporations) and community partners a deeper dive into the work the JobPath does. For the vast majority, we do not make a monetary ask in these story tours.

Instead, we do two things.

We ask them to spread the word about JobPath and we ask if we can put them on our email list. We have not had one person say no to the latter.

The process for inviting people to story tours is really simple. Staff encounter people in the community and if we sense a desire to learn more about what we do, we invite them. We've invited fellow nonprofits, foundations, corporations, elected officials, community members, among others.

We would like to eventually get to the place of having dedicated times for story tours; however, at this time we work with the invitee's schedule.

John: How has the story created a journey (stewardship) for the donor?

Frank: Remember, the story tour is the first step in the journey. They now know who we are, what we do, and what our outcomes are. This is critical information for them to know and share.

John: How has your story tours enhanced donor relationships? What percentage of donors have increased their support as a result of a story tour?

Frank: Story tours have significantly enhanced donor relationships primarily through our foundations, public funding, and corporate giving. For example, JobPath just received a $25,000 grant last week from Bank of America Charitable Foundation because of the story tour. Before the concept of the story tour, this foundation gave JobPath an average of about $15,000 per year. After inviting two representatives to come to a JobPath Story Tour, we were invited to apply for a $50,000 grant (in which we came in second but have been strongly encouraged to apply for again).

Then soon after, we were the only nonprofit to be asked to apply for a $25,000 grant which we received.

John: What are some common next steps you've seen donors take after participating in a story tour?

Frank: Because we ask potential donors to spread the word, that is exactly what they do. And it has been making an impact. There is a definite feeling that more people are learning about JobPath.

John: Tell me about your executive staff and board buy-in around the story tour. How important is their support and buy-in?

Frank: There is tremendous support for story tours. Their support and buy-in has been 100 percent. They understand the importance of communicating what we do to the larger community. And story tours do that in a very effective manner. In fact, potential board members are required to attend a story tour. New staff are required to attend a story tour during their on-boarding.

John: How has your story tours impacted your brand?

Frank: Story tours have become a part of JobPath. They have positively impacted our brand. In fact, one of our granters has modeled our story tours in recruiting partners for their organization. And JobPath is actually a component of this granter's story tour. A nonprofit's story within the granter's story. Very clever!

John: For nonprofits considering story tours as a way to encourage donors, what mistakes should they avoid? Or what tips, based on your experience, would you give to a novice?

Frank: Nonprofits should personalize their story tour the way they best see fit. They should also understand the story arc and how to use the story arc in their story tour. Understand how to move from introducing a personal client's story, but to leave it unfinished, next to explain how your nonprofit addresses and solves the problem (from a broad perspective), then to finish the story tour by finishing the personal client's story. It is also critical to introduce staff during the story tours. Story tours are all about personal connections. Don't sterilize story tours by making them robotic. Keep them intimate and personal.

PART SIX

Surrounding Yourself with CARE

Introduction

When you are told you have months to live, obviously your perspective on life completely changes. Mind did. I realized I have no control over what may come, and I certainly can't get all hung up on anything that happened in the past.

The only thing I have control over is this day. If I can practice healthy habits today, then I'll be more likely to live tomorrow, where I can repeat the same habits. This is the kind of attitude I have developed over the past two years of having cancer.

In this final section of the book, I will focus on the importance of caring for yourself and building an organizational culture where CARE comes naturally.

CHAPTER 27

Self-CARE Essentials for Nonprofits

One benefit or silver lining of having cancer is that I have developed a unique perspective on self-care. I've learned over the past two years how to take better care of my body and my mind every single day. As my cancer advances to the fourth stage, of course my goal is to maximize my health as much as possible so I can live a long quality life. Quality plus quantity is what I seek.

Before I had cancer, like many people who are cancer free, I could've taken my health for granted. Fortunately for me, I had a regular habit of exercising every single week. But, I felt if I don't make it to the gym this week, no problem, there's always next week.

But now I cannot afford to think that way. If I go one week without taking care of my health, I might severely deteriorate. This is true, especially when you are doing chemo, which can severely impair your health.

So cancer has forced me to focus on every single day. That's where I have control. I can't control tomorrow. I can only make the choices today to maximize my health as much as possible. If I do that again tomorrow, I'll be more likely to repeat the process again. Until I can't. In my experience, the best way to focus on self-care is to develop healthy daily habits.

With all that said, please keep in mind there are many books out there that are better than this one in terms of taking care of your health. But I will offer a few simple habits I try to practice every single day to maximize my health for as long as possible. Take what you like and leave the rest.

Water is life. When I don't drink enough water, all my systems get gunked up. Water is life. Water is motion. Without it, all systems within the body slow down, at least that's my experience. It impacts my digestion vitality and even clarity of thought. My goal every day is to drink at least two liters of water. I carry around a liter Nalgene bottle. I drink a full one before 1 pm and another before 6 pm. Ask your doctor what the right amount of water is for you.

Go outside. We are not machines, we are animals. We are not designed to slump in a cubicle for nine hours every day. This will cause your eventual decline in health. Evolution says that we need to get outside and move in nature. Look at the sky, look at the sun. Get your daily dose of vitamin D like every other diurnal animal on this planet. And if you're bald like me, your head is one big solar panel! If it's raining or snowing, get outside anyway. Again, 50,000 years ago, you would be outside all the time!

Close the laptop. Get outside and go for a walk. As a fourth stage cancer patient, walking every day is absolutely critical for my health. Exercising lowers fatigue, improves immune function, and creates a positive mental state. You don't have to have cancer to benefit from daily exercise!

Eat the rainbow. We've all read that the Mediterranean diet is the healthiest, or at least healthier than the Western diet. At Dana-Farber, a nutritionist once said to me, "Eat the rainbow." Eat a variety of healthy organic vegetables. Red ones, yellow ones, green ones, purple ones. Eat the rainbow.

Connect with a good friend. Isolation kills. It causes depression, suppressed immune function, and a host of other mental, spiritual, and physical problems. We cannot survive in isolation. Every day, I either talk on the phone or have coffee or lunch with a good friend. Good friends always leave you better than when they found you. In turn, encouraging a good friend positively expands your own state of being.

CHAPTER 28

A Self-CARE Interview with Beth Kanter

As I said, I am not an expert on self-care. I've learned the hard way through having cancer. That said, my very good friend Beth Kanter agreed to share her take on self-care for fundraisers. We had a wonderful discussion about self-care and what it really means. Beth is the co-author with Aliza Sherman of *The Happy, Healthy Nonprofit: Strategies for Impact Without Burnout.*

John: From a donor happiness perspective, how important is it that employees are happy? How does self-care impact what donors experience?

Beth: Let's face it, fundraising for a nonprofit can be stressful. According to a recent survey of fundraisers in 2019 by the Chronicle of Philanthropy, a vast majority feel they are working in a pressure cooker, leading to anxiety and unhappiness with the work.

The numbers are eye popping: 84 percent of fundraisers said they felt "tremendous pressure to succeed" in their role. And 55 percent said they "often feel unappreciated" in their work.

Fundraisers often have to work evening hours, attending fundraising events or meeting with donors, and often don't take off comp time due to the workloads. According to research, working overtime or "hero" hours at work is tied to a host of health problems and diseases. Believe it or not, Japan has a term for the effects of this type of work: Karōshi, or "death by overwork."

As a fundraiser, if you don't practice self-care to reduce your stress, it can lead to burnout or even worse. The World Health Organization has recently classified workplace burnout as an illness to call attention to the negative impact of work-related stress. Organizations have a big role in addressing burnout by paying attention to whether employees have a sense of community at work, strong social relationships, a collegial environment, a workload that's not too burdensome, a sense of purpose at work, and a healthy work-life balance.

Workplace burnout is when an employee or volunteer has reached the limit of physical and/or emotional strength. It then takes a toll on attitude and productivity and this can directly impact your relationship with your donor. Often fundraisers might attribute the impact from long hours, tight deadlines, and no resources. However, these are symptoms of a deeper organizational dysfunction, including lack of opportunities for advancement, heavy workloads, unrealistic job expectations, and long hours as factors that increased stress.

If you end up in the burnout bin, you are not good to anyone, not your family or your friends, your nonprofit, and especially to your donors. And, remember, the first phase of burnout is being passion-driven and so you might not realize you are burning out. Passion is not a sustainability fundraiser resource.

Fundraisers who practice self-care bolster their ability to deal with workplace stress and build better relationships with their donors. Self-care allows fundraisers to replenish their energy, energy that is needed to connect and be present with a donor.

John: What does it mean to connect with ourselves and how does that healthy connection allow us to better connect with others, whether it's co-workers, our boss, or donors?

Beth: Fundraisers can positively impact their work and life when they make a conscious commitment to, and form an intentional practice of, self-care. The goal is not to simply start scheduling isolated activities for yourself like taking a yoga class or eating chocolate. Your goal should be to make self-care a part of your life. Your self-care must be inseparable from your passion for fundraising as well as be an integral part of your organization's strategies and values.

It requires taking a holistic view of who you are and how you are, from head to toe, inside and out, to gauge what you are missing and where you are complete. You are more than your fundraising campaign goals. You bring far more to your organization than simply your skills. You need to honor all aspects of yourself—Physical, Mental, Emotional and Spiritual—and understand how failing to care for yourself opens the door to disease within you and that influences how you interact with your donors.

Self-care can directly affect your levels of happiness and health through Attention, Awareness, and Attendance.

- Attention to you, the individual, as an integral part of the whole organization.

- Awareness of issues or situations that are causing problems for you.

- Attendance to the root of the problems that are adversely affecting you.

Self-care isn't about a quick fix by doing an exercise class, a massage or an unplugged weekend—but any or all of those things can be incorporated into our lives, adopted as new habits, and become as essential to our day as brushing our teeth. Taking care of ourselves can result in a boost in organizational productivity because happier staff can relate better to others, cope better with stress, and experience more sustainable energy to apply to taking care of our donors. Bottom line: your self-care practices are good for you and your donors!

Self-care involves taking deliberate and consistent steps to prioritize your physical, mental and emotional health. Self-care is about enhancing your overall wellbeing, at work, at home and everyone you interact with, including your donors.

How you relate with yourself, with others, and with your surroundings and other elements can have a direct impact on your wellbeing. There are some fundamental areas of your life that deserve your attention. You can experience stress in each of these areas, and you can also apply self-care techniques in each area to better attend to your wellbeing and manage your stress levels. In my book, *The Happy, Healthy Nonprofit*, there are five areas to examine relationships and practice self-care. These include: self, others, environment, work, and technology.

When stressed out, you might find you have a "short fuse" or end up treating donor interaction as another annoying task versus with love and care. Even if you are able to reserve small pockets of patience for interacting with your donors, this is not the way you should be doing your work.

The way to get started is to change your relationship with yourself. If you pay attention to the wellness triad of sleep, nutrition, and exercise, this can help buffer you from burnout. With grounding, you can begin to incorporate important self-care practices such as mindfulness, spirituality, creativity, and reflection. The good news is that you don't need to carve out huge chunks of time to do this. You can weave moments of self-care mindful moments into your work day.

When you focus on your relationship with yourself, it has a positive impact with your relationships with others, including family, friends, co-workers and, of course, donors.

John: What role does appreciation play in self-care?

Beth: Another word for appreciation is being grateful. According to the Science of Gratitude Research Study, gratitude may be associated with many benefits for individuals, including better physical and psychological health, increased happiness and life satisfaction, decreased materialism, and more. A handful of studies suggest that more grateful people may be healthier, and other studies suggest that scientifically designed practices to increase gratitude can also improve people's health and encourage them to adopt healthier habits.

There are connections between gratitude and various elements of psychological well-being. In general, more grateful people are happier, more satisfied with their lives, less materialistic, and less likely to suffer from burnout. Additionally, some studies have found that consistent gratitude practices can increase people's happiness and overall positive mood.

So, how can you develop a gratitude practice? There are countless techniques you can apply to develop a gratitude practice, many of them catalogued by the Greater Good Magazine. Here are a few simple exercises to get you started:

- Reflect on the positive. Keep a one-sentence gratitude journal where you write one sentence a day noting what you are grateful for. This can help you stop taking things for granted.
- Write a "Gratitude Letter." Writing and then delivering a heartfelt letter of gratitude to someone you have never properly thanked can boost your sense of gratefulness but also strengthen your bond with them. Why send a handwritten thank you to your donors?
- Imagine a different life. Recall a positive experience in your lift and imagine how things would have turned out differently if that event did not occur.
- Take a mindful walk in nature. Observe the sights, sounds, and smells you encounter. Each time you notice something positive and wonderful, take a few minutes to absorb it and think about why you enjoy it.

Making appreciation part of your DNA will seep into your fundraising work and strengthen your bonds with your donor. If you appreciate life and are thankful, it sends out a positive energy that makes it easy to connect with others.

John: What is the value of building a mutually supportive community, or group of cohorts, in developing self-care?

Beth: While self-care is something we do for ourselves, when we go to work we are in a communal space. Creating a culture of resilience on your fundraising team or colleagues can help enhance your self-care efforts. One way to do this is to create a workplace or team rituals to nurture wellbeing.

Rituals are intentional small, tangible acts done routinely and carry meaning. Rituals have been performed for centuries and are an important part of human history—from religious ceremonies to common rituals like saying hello or shaking hands. Rituals are also used by professionals to boost personal productivity because rituals capitalize on our brains' ability to direct our behavior on autopilot, allowing us to reach our goals even when we are distracted or preoccupied with other things.

Workplaces are tapping into the power of ritual to create a sense of community, build relationships in the workplace and reduce stress. And if that wasn't enough, rituals can also encourage innovation by reducing the fear of failure.

If you think about it, our nonprofit organizations already have rituals—from the boring everyday activities like coffee breaks to larger events such as annual meetings and holiday parties. Now that we know what the research says about the benefits of rituals, nonprofit leaders should view the creation and fostering of rituals as essential, whether for the entire organization, your department, or team.

Here are a few examples:

- Completion of Fundraising Campaigns or Big Project: Did your organization just complete a successful fundraising campaign or maybe you just launched a new web presence or database. Celebrate that milestone with anything festive that fits your organization's values, is inclusive, and everyone finds enjoyable. This could be a pizza or taco party or giving comp time.

- Employee of the Week or Month: Did someone on your team or in your organization make an extraordinary contribution to your organization's programs and went above and beyond to make it a success? Having a formal and consistent way to recognize staff who work hard can motivate others. One organization has a silly banana statue that they give to the "Top Banana" for the month. Others have created a "whiteboard of love" with written praise or staff accomplishments, provided reserved parking space, or take time to praise staff at monthly meetings. Of course, a raise or bonus is nice, but it is the public acknowledge that helps build community.

- Lunch and Learns and Field Trips: Inviting outside experts to lunch at your office to learn about their work can make professional development an experience that also builds community. Another way to promote learning is to organize a field trip to visit your organization's programs in the field or another organization to learn from their work.

- Recognize Birthdays and Work Anniversaries: Look for a fun way to celebrate birthdays and work anniversaries. Give them a cake or have everyone sign a birthday card with a small gift. You can decorate their office door, give them a birthday hat, or sing happy birthday. One nonprofit gives the employee a comp day off on their birthday or work anniversary. Some workplaces also celebrate the birth of children and weddings. And, upon the death of a loved one, find an appropriate way to express sympathy in the workplace. All this can help humanize your workplace.

It is also important to think about what will make a ritual stick. Why will people want to participate? Can it start organically and catch on, or will people look to certain leaders to model it first? Designing a ritual that will sustain over time requires tuning in to the organization's existing culture, beliefs, and behaviors. One important step is to get feedback and ideas from staff to help create that important buy-in.

There are many examples of workplace rituals that your nonprofit can initiate. A well designed ritual will reinforce mind-sets and behaviors in a way that feels authentic to the nonprofit's mission and people.

John: How can we encourage ourselves, or give ourselves permission to do self-care?

Beth: The first step is to change the way you may be framing self-care. It is not selfish. It doesn't mean that you are weak or lazy. It does mean that you understand that in the face of the challenging work that nonprofit fundraisers tackle every day, you need to be unapologetic about self-care.

Start with one self-care activity, make it a small step and find the time in your daily routine that makes the best sense to start. Then train that cycle until your self-care is second nature. Get started, and after a few weeks, you will begin to notice the benefits.

By practicing self-care, you are not only taking care of yourself but also taking care of your organization's mission and all of your donors.

CHAPTER 29

Building a Culture of CARE

Tom Ahern calls it the Ignorance Ceiling.

I've got countless bumps and dents on my bald little head from smacking up against the ignorance ceiling.

Smart marketing folks at a nonprofit and I will develop a strategy we know will work. We did the research, mapped out a plan, developed story structures, and created a social media strategy.

Then inevitably I'll get the phone call from my battered and bruised client: "My boss thinks it's too risky. They want to repeat the campaign we did last year. I know it didn't really work, but they don't want to take any risks at this time. I'm really sorry."

Tom writes in his (must read) book, *If Only You'd Known...You Would Have Raised So Much More:* "You have someone above you who gets to say yay or nay. And that person (boss, board member or committee) has no clue what they're talking about."

In my experience, the ignorance ceiling is the biggest issue nonprofits face. It prevents them from advancing with digital, connecting with donors, taking risks, raising more money. Front line staff are not the problem. Grunts get it. Executives and board members are often the ones who don't get it. I've seen countless good ideas obliterated because someone in power was arrogant, ignorant, or too lazy to keep up with how donors want to connect.

For CARE to be truly effective, the entire organization must exude a CARE culture. It can look like this.

Connect. A willingness to connect. Beth Kanter calls this the Networked Nonprofit. Connect means to understand that every single individual plays an important role in the success of the organization. And not just individuals inside the organization.

Appreciate. A nonprofit that has a spirit of gratitude and appreciation for employees will raise more money. But gratitude is not just a nice feeling, smiles, and saying thank you in the hallway. This means paying them well, creating a positive work environment, and offering competitive employee benefits, including health insurance.

Reply. Nonprofits that have executives who embrace an open door policy, seeking dialogue and seeking to learn from everyone in the organization, will raise more money. When people feel heard and their voice matters they will be more committed to the work. If an executive asks you for proof on this, just know that you are staring at the ignorance ceiling.

Encourage. Leaders should create an environment where employees want to go to work and feel a common bond around a shared mission. Staff will be much happier and committed personally as if it's their own mission.

Mary Cahalane writes in a recent article, "What Your Fundraisers are Saying That You Need to Hear," about research that reflects the ignorance ceiling. "Many of us in the nonprofit sector put ourselves last. The mission is everything, and we're all just worker bees. Even worker bees need nourishment!"

Mary shares these points from the Harris poll:

- This is a high-pressure, low appreciation career. (I know, you're shocked!)
- Staff and board don't understand fundraising.
- Fundraising work with tremendous pressure in tight timelines. (Stress much?)
- There is a lack of trust that hinders fundraisers' performance and satisfaction.
- Too many organizations don't have a culture of philanthropy.
- Fundraisers deal with poor management and communication.
- And there is not enough investment in fundraisers or fundraising.

Change can happen, but it will happen faster and more effectively if it happens internally and at the top of your nonprofit, not just in your external communications.

CHAPTER 30

A CARE Interview with Jillian Vorce

A very good friend of mine, Jillian Vorce, and I recently discussed the CARE framework and how organizations can begin to change their culture from CAREless too CAREful. Jillian is an author of *20/20 Mind Sight*, an advisor, speaker, and founder of The Jillian Group. With over 20 years in management and leadership consulting, Jillian's energy, intuitive charm, and get-to-the-grit wit have inspired senior-level executives, business owners, and creatives alike to bring their A-game to life and business.

John: A big part of the idea of customer care—and for our purposes, donor care—is connecting, appreciating, responding to, and encouraging people to take their next step, whatever their next step is. And a critical part of creating a happy crowd of surefooted donors is this idea of oneness in the organizational leadership attitude—the idea that what exists in the hearts and minds of leaders penetrates through every layer of their organizations, inspiring and spreading people to bring their best to the cause.

Now, we've all experienced nonprofits with beautifully written fundraising appeals, inspiring websites, and the incredibly donor-centric communications—only to be extremely disappointed with the people behind the paper. This happens all too often, and it happens when a leader's heart isn't in it. And when a leader's heart isn't in it, what is the rest of the team to do? Instead of a care culture, you get disconnection. Instead of relationships, you get mailing lists. Instead of ownership and pride, you get a general lack of direction. And so the first question really is, within leadership or within a culture, where do leaders really begin to solve this problem?

Jillian: I think there's only one place to begin—exactly where they are. It reminds me of what I call the Concept of One Degree. There's this great video on YouTube that talks about how water goes from boiling to steam at 212 degrees. And boiling water can make pasta or sterilize bottles—which is great—but when it becomes steam, it can power a locomotive. All from moving just one degree.

Anytime you're looking at change management for any organization, whether it's a cultural shift, a changing of the guard, or a leadership mindset, it's pretty typical to bring in an outside organization that will lay out all these things that have to change. And, just as typically, compliance never happens. People aren't able to execute because there's just too much to bite off. For an organization to have all of the pieces except for the most critical—their leadership—they'll be stuck on the tracks at 211 degrees. And until they recognize the problem—a general lack of awareness and engagement—they'll continue to sit.

Approaching it from the top down has most likely been done, so perhaps that critical one-degree change might be to approach the challenge from a different angle and open it up for conversation. And this is important practice—engaging with employees is really the same thing as engaging with donors. After all, they are both stakeholders. If you can empower people on one side of the equation, it will penetrate through.

To your point, I feel like successful leaders do that. Successful leaders empower their people to maximize their productivity by understanding that—more than money and medical benefits and free coffee—people want to feel seen and heard and valued, and the more they are seen and heard and valued, the more energy they'll put into what they're doing. And the greater the output, the faster an organization can achieve change under its own steam. And you can achieve that one critical degree of change just by changing the hows and whos of the brainstorming and decision-making process.

John: Yeah, that's brilliant. I love it. That penetration you spoke of is what I call the Law of Care. Like gravity, the Law of Care basically says greatness has to start within the hearts and minds of the leaders. Then it goes to the organizational culture, then to the employees, and finally the customers. Given the Law of Care, it's impossible to have happy donors if your employees are unhappy.

Celebrating this care takes connection, appreciation, responsiveness, and engagement. What does it mean to have a culture of connection within an organization given that employees and donors both want to feel connected to the products, brands, and the causes they invest in?

Jillian: With connection, a few things come to mind. One is proximity. How close are we physically and emotionally to the work, the people, and the impact we're trying to make? Are we in the same room? Are we making eye contact? Can they tell if I'm not paying attention? Do they care?

The second thing is recognition. Connecting with people these days is both hard and remarkably easy. Everyone's in a hurry, no one is watching where they are going or looking at who they are talking to. So when someone is truly present with us, it blows us away. That's a skill I never knew I had—I call it being a professional human—until I realized that what came so easily to me—putting away my phone, getting good and curious, asking the not-so-obvious questions, and thoughtfully responding to answers—was so hard for some people. We as humans sometimes forget how good this type of presence feels and how nice it is to be seen and recognized.

Connection comes from heightened awareness. I happen to love making connections. It's basically just demonstrating to others that I'm actually here. I'm paying attention. I'm present. I'm going to remember something about you, and I'm going to remind you that I haven't forgotten about what makes you, you.

John: You've done your homework.

Jillian: Yeah, I've done my homework, and I'm deliberately here. What a lot of nonprofits forget is that while their causes are important, so are their donors. It's easy for nonprofits to keep repeating what they do, how they help, and why it's so critical. But what about that donor or that employee? What's going on with them?

John: So how do you connect those pieces?

Jillian: It's two simple things, really: Ask some darn good questions and be prepared to shed some genuine light on their responses. The answer to that connection is hidden in their answers—what will they bring to light? What will you bring? Most people don't just want to be seen—they want to feel seen, which means you're giving them recognition in a way that they truly value. Most people handle that kind of recognition pretty awkwardly. They'll brush it off. "I'm just the secretary. I'm just this. I'm just that."

Don't let them get away with it. They're too important. It's your job as a leader to remind them and hold them accountable to their talents, skills, and the good work they do. Once they truly understand how much they matter, they can't help but feel more enthusiastic about and connected to the work and to you as a leader. It's your Law of Care in the present tense.

How does communication flow? How are ideas shared? How are you giving them feedback? What are you doing to celebrate the people in your organization and your life? What are we doing so that people See each other? Do other people have the opportunity to share or to lead meetings or to come up with ideas for the new fundraiser or the next event?

John: That makes me think of the point you made about being a professional human being because part of that is also this basic act of saying, "Thank you." And that's what brings us to the next part of a CARE Culture—appreciation. How have you incorporated appreciation with your relationships and how has it changed them?

Jillian: Yes, appreciation. This one feels like another very basic one, but it's one most of us understand and do almost without thinking. I mean, most of us know how to handle ourselves socially. We're good students. We show up. We know what we're supposed to say. And there's a lot of autopilot that goes with that. We know when we're supposed to say, "Bless you" when someone sneezes, "Happy Birthday" when the cake comes out, "I'm good" when someone asks you how you've been.

An amazing thing happens, though, when you disconnect from autopilot and start getting a feel for the controls. That's what engagement is, after all—putting more of yourself and others into the conversation. Don't just say "Bless You." Smile when you do it. Tell the birthday girl you're happy she's on the planet. And don't just say "Thank you." Tell them why it matters. "Your review meant a lot to me." "Look what we've been able to do because of what you've done and who you are." Put their contribution into context.

John: And like we were talking about before, appreciation increases the value of that relationship. So essentially, appreciation is about recognizing the value that that person has brought to the relationship.

Now, third is the idea of Reply, which means allowing employees and donors to give feedback. The research shows that donors are actually more likely to give if they feel heard, which is why it's important to create an environment where there are plenty of opportunities for people to feel that their voice matters.

There's a great question I always recommend that my clients ask when someone gives—"What made you decide to give today?" Very simple. At that moment, you reinforce that act, you lower donor remorse, and it lets your donor put more skin in the game.

Jillian: Yes, and maybe don't stop there. "What is it about our organization? Is there a personal connection that you have? Is this something that you've been through or feel a connection with?"

I feel like the more you know about your donors, the more equipped you are to shine a light on what makes them so vital to your organization. And the companies that are detailed and deliberate about that data are the organizations that are going to win—because they'll know how to create a donor experience that actually aligns with what people are so desperately seeking. So never stop asking them in-the-moment, relevant questions. On the donor side, hands down, it needs to be about that, like, "Why are you here? How do you want to help? What else are you interested in?" Get them to see how they would contribute. Do they have other aspirations? Do they want to be involved in a greater capacity? Get them to see themselves doing the real work.

John: And also, that culture of personal connection gets shared throughout the organization. So it's not like an executive director has to meet with every single employee. But let's say the executive director stops in the mailroom and talks to the person sorting the mail, and saying, "Hey. How's it going? How's your family?" and can make that personal connection, that's enough to have that person say, "Oh wow. The executive director knows who I am!"

And then they say something to their coworkers. And they may tell their friends, and people start saying, "I want to work for an organization that truly cares about their people." Those stories get shared and that's how culture grows, both inward and outward. That's why I say it's like Oneness. The Law of Care says that when you care about one person deeply, you can care about everybody deeply throughout the organization because it's reflected throughout the organization.

Once you have that care in place, you now have personal connections with a personal stake in the game. And that's why it's having a strong organizational vision—one everyone can participate in—is so important. Because that personal stake isn't just what they are getting out of it, but what they're putting into it and where you as an organization and as a leader are going with it. And you better know where you are going.

Jillian: It's funny, the moment you talk about that, the word that comes to mind for me is humility. And I think of that word because it's easy to be all excited and warm and fuzzy when things go right, but it's critical to have humility when things aren't so rosy. What happens as an organization when we don't meet our goals? What happens when an event is a bust or we lose a major donor or we put our eggs in the wrong basket? I feel like there's just as much good that can come from something that goes wrong, especially from a leadership standpoint.

John: It's like Cyndi Lauper, the true colors come out.

Jillian: There you go. The times when things go wrong are the true-color test of any organization.

Who wails? Who bails? Who sails? The leaders that really capture the heart of an organization are the first ones to say, "Ok, what did we do well? What could we have done differently?" Great leaders are always hungry for feedback. Companies with strong visions can't get enough of it. Why? Because when the vision is too important, feedback becomes just another way to win. You can be very matter-of-fact about it. There are no negative feelings. People want to be a part of an organization that knows where they're going, even if they don't crush it all the time. Because no matter what, they keep moving forward.

John: Yeah, yeah. And if you don't talk about things like that, things go bad. Doubt sinks in. Trust goes out the window. When the chemistry is off in an organization, everyone feels it. People are afraid to make mistakes or take the ball, and they stop speaking up, even when it matters. That's when you know the CARE is gone.

Jillian: Right. And it can affect even your really committed employees if you're not careful. So part of the trick is to recognize that lackluster results and mistakes and misfires happen. They are a fact. So treat them factually. There's good news. There's bad news. What can we learn about it?

The goal is to create an "own it" culture of personal awareness, responsibility, and accountability, so finger-pointing gets replaced by hand-raising. Say it out loud so they can hear you: "I had this idea. I really believed it was going to work out. The numbers didn't bear out. Here's what I learned." And if leaders want their employees to step up to the plate, they better model how to act when life tosses those curveballs. Own those ball drops honestly. Teach your teams the value of asking for help, catching mistakes, or expressing concerns. As a CEO, I'd much rather learn about a problem when it's manageable! Cultures who are afraid to fail end up failing everyone, including the mission, and that's a shame. Because failure isn't an option—it's a part of life. How you deal with it is the true test.

CHAPTER 31

Some Final Advice on Moving Forward

I hope you've been inspired by this book to change the way you communicate with your donors. But it's possible that I've given you too much to think about. To help you take the next step, consider the Pareto Principle.

The Pareto Principle, or the 80:20 rule, was named after an Italian pea farmer named Pareto. Pareto discovered that 80 percent of his peas came from 20 percent of the pods in his garden. Today, the Pareto Principle is used in almost every facet of business, from human resources to manufacturing to sales, and of course marketing.

In fact, the Pareto Principle itself follows the Pareto Principle in that it's one of the most useful concepts you will ever employ in marketing and fundraising. In other words, out of all marketing and fundraising principles you will ever use, 20 percent of those concepts will most definitely include the Pareto Principle!

Which of your plants produce the most peas?

If you look at your own fundraising and marketing efforts, you'll find that:

- 20 percent of your donors give 80 percent of your fundraising revenue
- 20 percent of your fundraising campaigns raise to 80 percent of your annual revenue
- 20 percent of your advertising accounts for 80 percent of the acquired donors

Nonprofits that thrive tend to focus on the pods that produce 80 percent of the peas.

How can you improve your marketing and fundraising ROI using this same principle? Here are a few examples of how to think like a pea farmer:

1. Which email messages raise the most money? Undoubtedly, nonprofits get a significant amount of online donor conversations via email. Using the Pareto Principle, you'll find that 20 percent of your email campaigns produce 80 percent of the donations. Analyze your email conversions and figure out how to apply these email strategies to other campaigns.

2. Which Facebook posts drive the most engagement? Facebook has completely changed the way nonprofits raise money. Instead of having to hunt for potential donors, potential donors hear about nonprofits from their Facebook friends. Maximizing Facebook ROI means focusing your Facebook campaigns on the topics and interests that engage the most fans. For example, with Facebook Insights you can easily discover the 20 percent of your posts that drive 80 percent of your sharing.

3. Which marketing campaigns drive the most event registrants? Following the Pareto Principle, 20 percent of your event marketing generates 80 percent of the event registrants. Using Google Analytics, you can discover the campaigns that drive the most registrants. Once you figure this out, you can then focus 80 percent of your resources on the top 20 percent of your event marketing campaigns.

As you can see, the Pareto Principle can be used in a number of ways for your nonprofit. But however you decide to use the 80:20 rule, keep in mind that it requires two mindsets:

Discovery: Which pods are producing 80 percent of your peas? Using analytics (email, website, donor stats, etc) will help you discover the key 20 percent. For example, which fundraising stories drive 80 percent of your new donor conversions?

Effort: How will you grow more peas? Once you discover your key 20 percent, how will you adjust your marketing and fundraising strategies to get even more from that 20 percent? For example, you might develop a donor recognition campaign specifically for 20 percent of your donors that give 80 percent of your revenue.

In short, use the Pareto Principle to find the CAREful marketing and fundraising efforts that produce the most impact for your nonprofit specifically. Applying this principle to donor retention will mean focusing more of your resources on a donor experience after they make that first gift, not before.

I also want you to remember something else too: perfection slows everything down. Perfect can never be agreed upon. Perfect never gets done.

Are you daunted by perfectionism? If so, here are a few ways to tame the perfectionist in you:

1. View everything as a draft, especially content marketing. Publish the work, measure the results, edit as necessary, and repeat.

2. Define your goals. The more clear you are about your goals, the less likely you'll waste time.

3. Define "the 80 percent." Be clear about the items you need to complete to finish the project. Eighty percent and done is better than 100 percent perfect and never done.

4. Know when a good idea has gone stale. All ideas have a shelf life. If a week or so has gone by without any action towards your idea, maybe it wasn't a good idea.

5. Embrace mistakes. The best, most savvy nonprofits still trip and fall. Mistakes have made them stronger, quicker, and smarter.

Done is better than perfect.

Conclusion

Buddhism talks of being "one with everything." And whether you are a Buddhist or not, I think we can agree that we are all connected in a big story called "humanity." Our humanity—our oneness—allows us to remove the barriers that separate.

Together, you and I change our world. I feel a tremendous sense of appreciation for my life—gratitude for every moment. Cancer has enabled me dramatically to transform how I perceive the world. It has enriched how I respond to my loved ones and dear friends.

My Buddhist beliefs help bring out the more positive forces in my life. I've thought a lot about what my mission is with this cancer. I've wondered, "How can I turn this poison into medicine in my life?" The truth is, I'm using this cancer to encourage you. I want to use my suffering to inspire you to live every day well so you can make the world a better place.

My final wish for you is that by following my donor "CARE" advice—the culmination of my life's work—you'll attract added donations from existing donors . . . see your retention rates reach new heights . . . and attract passionate new supporters. But above all, I want you to practice self-care every single day. Make good choices to maximize your health. Embrace and appreciate your loved ones. After all, the only thing you can control is this moment.

And now, my friend, I must pass the torch to you. Carry it well.

References

Part One

Introduction
Seinfeld script, http://seinfeldscripts.com/TheAlternateSide.htm

Hyken, Shep. 2018. Businesses Lose $75 Billion Due To
Poor Customer Service. https://www.forbes.com/sites/
shephyken/2018/05/17/businesses-lose-75-billion-due-to-poor-
customer-service/#262b019716f9

Fundraising Effectiveness Project, http://afpfep.org/

Chapter 1
DonorPerfect. *Five Reasons Why a Monthly Giving Program Will
Benefit Your Organization.* https://www.philanthropy.com/paid-
article/five-reasons-why-a-monthly-giv/41

Sargeant, Adrian and Elaine Jay. 2011. *Building Donor Loyalty: The
Fundraiser's Guide to Increasing Lifetime Value.* JB.

Chapter 2
GiveCentral. 2015. *Predictions for Nonprofit Giving.* https://www.
givecentral.org/nonprofit-surveys

Sargeant, Adrian and Jay, Elaine. 2011. *Building Donor Loyalty: The
Fundraiser's Guide to Increasing Lifetime Value.* JB.

Bloomerang. Charities That Focus on Donor Retention Will Change the World. https://bloomerang.co/blog/charities-that-focus-on-retention-will-change-the-world/

Craver, Roger. 2014. *Retention Fundraising: The New Art and Science of Keeping Your Donors for Life.* Emerson & Church.

Chapter 3

Bloomerang. Charities That Focus on Donor Retention Will Change the World. https://bloomerang.co/blog/charities-that-focus-on-retention-will-change-the-world/

Chapter 5

Ferriss, Timothy. 2009. *The 4-Hour Workweek: Escape 9-5, Live Anywhere, and Join the New Rich.* Harmony Books.

Godin, Seth. 2007. *Purple Cow: Transform Your Business by Being Remarkable.* Penguin Books.

Walker, Rob and Glenn, Joshua. Significant Objects Project. http://significantobjects.com/

Saving Private Ryan script. https://www.moviequotedb.com/movies/saving-private-ryan/quote_20721.html

Frankl, Viktor E. 1946. *Man's Search for Meaning.* Beacon Press.

PART TWO

Introduction

Angelou, Maya. Quoted in *Why We Write* By Vikas Shah. https://www.goodreads.com/quotes/652190-we-write-for-the-same-reason-that-we-walk-talk

Morris, Desmond. 1988. *Catlore.* Crown Publishing Group.

Chapter 6

Harari, Yuval Noah. 2019. *Sapiens: a Brief History of Humankind.*

Vintage.

Gottschall, Jonathan. 2013. *The Storytelling Animal: How Stories Make Us Human*. Houghton Mifflin Harcourt.

Charity: water. 2014. "The Woman Who Fell Down the Well." *Medium*. https://medium.com/charity-water/the-woman-who-fell-down-the-well-5e72d68d7e9b

Zak, Paul. 2015. "Why Inspiring Stories Make Us React: The Neuroscience of Narrative." *Cerebrum*. https://www.ncbi.nlm.nih.gov/pmc/articles/PMC4445577/

Chapter 7

San Francisco Zoo. *Adopt a Lion*. http://www.sfzoo.org/support/donate/adopt/adopt-lion.html

Chapter 8

Slovic, Paul. 2007. "If I look at the mass I will never act: Psychic numbing and genocide." *Judgement and Decision Making*. http://journal.sjdm.org/7303a/jdm7303a.htm

Ellinger, Nick. 2018. "TESTING: When A/B Tests Attack (your results)." *The Agitator*. http://agitator.thedonorvoice.com/testing-when-a-b-tests-attack-your-results/

Humane Society of Northeast Georgia. Habersham Rescue. https://www.humanesocietyofnortheastgeorgia.org/habrescueupdate/

Chapter 9

Mercy For Animals. *Choose Veg*. https://chooseveg.com/

Baer, Jay. 2014. *Youtility: Why Smart Marketing Is about Help Not Hype*. Portfolio.

Fight Colorectal Cancer ambassadors. https://fightcolorectalcancer.org/join-fight/raise-awareness/

ambassador-training-program/

PART THREE

Introduction
Daisaku, Ikeda. Quote cited in *Ikeda Quotes*. https://www.
ikedaquotes.org/human-relationships/humanrelationships224.
html?quotes_start=49

Dispenza, Joe. 2018. "Processing a Biological Upgrade." *Dr. Joe Dispenza's Blog.*

Blog post, https://drjoedispenza.net/blog/change/processing-a-biological-upgrade/

Chapter 12
Emmons, Robert A. and McCullough, Michael E.. 2003. *Counting Blessings Versus Burdens: An Experimental Investigation of Gratitude and Subjective Well-Being in Daily Life.* https://greatergood.berkeley.edu/images/application_uploads/Emmons-CountingBlessings.pdf

Carpenter, Kathryn, Day, Harriet, and Sargeant, Adrian. 2018. *Learning to Say Thank-You: The Role of Donor Acknowledgments.* https://www.philanthropy-centre.org/wp-content/uploads/2018/11/Acknowledgment-Report-061118.pdf

Chapter 13
Maxwell, Cameron. 2017. "How Ozzy was Fired from Black Sabbath." *Medium.* https://medium.com/@cmaxwell70/how-ozzy-was-fired-from-black-sabbath-9b462ba83b35

Chapter 16
The Humane Society of Northeast Georgia.
https://www.humanesocietyofnortheastgeorgia.org/

PART FOUR

Introduction
Goldstein, Meredith. *Love Letters.* https://loveletters.boston.com/
Polar Bears International. https://polarbearsinternational.org/

Chapter 18
Craver, Roger. 2014. *Retention Fundraising: The New Art and Science of Keeping Your Donors for Life.* Emerson & Church.
Bloomerang. 2018. *Donor Commitment Survey Template.* https://bloomerang.co/resources/templates/donor-commitment-survey-template

Chapter 19
Craver, Roger. 2014. *Retention Fundraising: The New Art and Science of Keeping Your Donors for Life.* Emerson & Church.
Jung, Carl. 1928. "The Relations between the Ego and the Unconscious." *CW 7: Two Essays on Analytical Psychology.*
The New York Times Customer Insight Group. 2011. *The Psychology of Sharing: Why do People Share Online?* http://templatelab.com/the-psychology-of-sharing/

Chapter 20
Frankel, David, director. 2011. *The Big Year.* 20th Century Fox.
Urban Dictionary. https://www.urbandictionary.com/define.php?term=hater

Chapter 21
Museum of Fine Arts, Boston. https://www.mfa.org/
Kanter, Beth, and Allison H. Fine. 2010. *The Networked Nonprofit: Connecting with Social Media to Drive Change.* San Francisco: Jossey-Bass.

Kanter, Beth, Katie Delahaye Paine, and William T. Paarlberg. 2012. *Measuring the Networked Nonprofit: Using Data to Change the World*. San Francisco: Jossey-Bass.

Chapter 22
Food For Free. https://foodforfree.org/

Part Five

Introduction
Ikeda, Daisaku. 2000. *The Way of Youth: Buddhist Common Sense for Handling Life*. https://www.amazon.com/Way-Youth-Buddhist-Handling-Questions/dp/0967469708

Chapter 23
Autoblog staff. 2018. History's 10 Best Selling Cars of All Time. *Autoblog*.
https://www.autoblog.com/photos/historys-10-bestselling-cars-of-all-time/
Ford, Henry and Crowther, Samuel. 1922. *My Life and Work*. Garden City Publishing Company, Inc.
Bluefrog Fundraising. https://bluefroglondon.com/

Chapter 24
The Blackbaud Institute. *Sustainers in Focus*. https://institute.blackbaud.com/sustainers-in-focus/
Growth in Giving Initiative. 2018. *2018 Fundraising Effectiveness Survey Report*. http://afpfep.org/wp-content/uploads/2018/04/2018-Fundraising-Effectiveness-Survey-Report.pdf.
Waasdorp, Erica. 2012. *Monthly Giving: the Sleeping Giant*. BookBaby.

2019. "3 Ways to Spotlight Your Monthly Giving Program on Giving Tuesday." *DonorPerfect Blog.* https://www.donorperfect.com/giving-tuesday/monthly-gift-strategy

Mercy for Animals. *Investigator Allies.* https://mercyforanimals.org/

Chapter 25

Joyaux, Simone. 2016. "Keep Your Donors: It's the Right Thing to Do—And It Makes You More Money." *Nonprofit Quarterly.* https://nonprofitquarterly.org/keep-donors-right-thing-makes-money/

Love, Jay. 2015. "The Single Simplest Way To Improve Fundraising Results Is…." *Bloomerang Blog.* https://bloomerang.co/blog/the-single-simplest-way-to-improve-fundraising-results-is

Chapter 26

JobPath. https://www.jobpath.net/

Chapter 28

Kanter, Beth, and Aliza Sherman. 2017. *The Happy, Healthy Nonprofit: Strategies for Impact without Burnout.* Wiley.

Josyln, Heather. 2019. "Why Fundraisers Leave, and How to Keep Them." *The Chronicle of Philanthropy.*

World Health Organization. https://www.who.int/

Greater Good Science Center. 2018. *The Science of Gratitude.* https://ggsc.berkeley.edu/images/uploads/GGSC-JTF_White_Paper-Gratitude-FINAL.pdf

Greater Good Magazine. https://greatergood.berkeley.edu/

Chapter 29

Ahern, Tom. 2019. *If Only You'd Known…You Would Have Raised So Much More.* Emerson & Church Publishers

Cahalane, Mary. "What Your Fundraisers Are Saying That You Need to Hear." *Hands On Fundraising.* https://mcahalane.com/what-your-fundraisers-are-saying-that-you-need-to-hear/

AFP and *Chronicle of Philanthropy.* 2019. "Fundraisers Satisfied with Many Aspects of Their Job, But Half Likely to Leave Current Position in Two Years." *AFP Blog.* https://afpglobal.org/fundraisers-satisfied-many-aspects-their-job-half-likely-leave-current-position-two-years

Chapter 30

Fragasso, Philip M., and Jillian Vorce. 2016. *20/20 Mind Sight.* Contigo Press.

Made in the USA
Middletown, DE
20 March 2020

86896127R00163